CONGO DIARY
and Other Uncollected Pieces

CONGO DIARY

and Other Uncollected Pieces

by Joseph Conrad

———————◆————————

Edited and with Comments by
Zdzisław Najder

DOUBLEDAY & COMPANY, INC., GARDEN CITY, NEW YORK   1978

Library of Congress Cataloging in Publication Data

Conrad, Joseph, 1857–1924.
Congo diary and other uncollected pieces.

"Biographical bibliography": p. 152.
I. Najder, Zdzisław. II. Title.
PR6005.O4A6   1978   823'.9'12   [B]
ISBN: 0-385-00771-x
Library of Congress Catalog Card Number 72–89333

Contents

Introduction

This volume contains all of Joseph Conrad's writings intended for publication which hitherto have not been included in the so-called "collected editions."[1]

Conrad's reputation as one of the greatest modern writers in English seems by now to be fully established. To have his entire literary output gathered and accessible surely does not require justification. Although none of these uncollected and unpublished pieces represents a major achievement, and several of them are quite trivial, all are of considerable interest to any Conrad scholar or admirer. But up till now these texts have been obtainable only in rare editions, or in the files of old English periodicals—or not at all.

The idea of publishing this supplementary volume occurred to me in the course of my work on a collected edition of Conrad's writings in Polish translation. It was while gathering materials for that edition—the first of its kind in any language—that I brought together all texts contained in the present book.

Professors Frederick R. Karl and Thomas Moser read parts of the manuscript and gave me their helpful and encouraging advice. Harvard College Library kindly permitted me to publish the manuscripts of the two Conrad Congo notebooks in their possession; Captain Józef Miłobędzki helped me in deciphering some passages in the second notebook.

Acknowledgment is also made gratefully to the Beinecke Rare Book and Manuscript Library, Yale University, for permission to publish the drafts of Conrad's speech at a meeting of the Lifeboat Institution.

With the exception of *The Nature of a Crime,* written by Ford Madox Ford (Hueffer) in collaboration with Conrad, which is placed last, all items are ordered chronologically. As they do not form any coherent set, I discuss each of them in separate introductory comments.

Zdzisław Najder

Note to Introduction

1. However, dramatic adaptations of "Tomorrow," "Because of the Dollars," and *The Secret Agent* are not included, since they were intended primarily for the stage. They were published in a separate volume in 1934.

CONGO DIARY
and Other Uncollected Pieces

Conrad's stay in the Congo (12 June–4 December 1890) is one of the most important periods of his life. Even if we question as excessive the claim of his first biographer, G. Jean-Aubry, that the journey to the Congo shaped Conrad's philosophical outlook,[1] we must recognize the enormous physical and moral impact of these six months. Conrad signed in Brussels a contract to serve for three years as an officer on river steamboats belonging to the Société Anonyme pour le Commerce du Haut-Congo. He left Europe full of energy and thrilling expectations, with ideas about a "civilizing mission."[2] He returned gravely ill, never to regain fully his good health, disillusioned, with memories to be used later in his most famous story, "Heart of Darkness," and in another bitter denunciation of colonialism, "An Outpost of Progress."

From this period there survive a few letters and also a unique document, the so-called "Congo Diary." The manuscript consists of two notebooks. The first, untitled, is an actual diary, kept by Conrad during his trek from Matadi to Kinshasa between 13 June and 1 August. This part was published (with errors and rather spotty annotation) by Richard Curle in 1926 and included in the volume *Last Essays*. The second, entitled by Conrad "Up-river Book" and commenced on board the steamer *Roi des Belges* on 3 August 1890, does not preserve the form of a diary—there are only four dates, although it spans sixteen days—and contains almost exclusively notes, instructions and sketches concerning navigation up the Congo, at that time a not-too-frequented and only recently explored river. The second notebook was not published by Curle because, according to him, "it has no personal or literary interest."[3] This I believe is an exaggerated statement; still, since Curle's verdict, no Conrad scholar seems to have looked into the "Up-river Book."

The Congo notes constitute one of Conrad's earliest writings in English and reflect, if not his command of the language (his third), then at least his characteristic difficulties with it. These would come from two sides at once: from the Polish, which was his native language, the only one he used daily for his first seventeen years, and the one in which in 1890 he wrote most of his letters; and from the French, which he learned as a child, mastered during his stay in France in 1874–78 and, of course, used in the Congo. And his difficulties were threefold: choice of words, spelling, and grammar, particularly syntax.

Spelling mistakes are, of course, both most obvious and most trivial. Usually, not only in the notebooks, but in Conrad manuscripts in general, they stemmed from a similarity between an English and a French (differently spelled) word; and so he would write "ressemble" for "resemble," "mentionned" for "mentioned," and so on. Some, like the persistent "lays" and "laying" for "lies" and "lying" (found also, for instance, in a letter to Garnett of 15 March 1895), arise from the intricacies of English conjugation. The really exotic ones, like "andulating" for "undulating," can be explained only by reference to the rules of Polish spelling and pronunciation.

In his choice of words, Conrad would sometimes fail to realize the difference of meaning between similar-looking French and English words: hence "accidented" in the sense of "uneven." In grammar, the pressure of Polish seems to have been stronger throughout his writing career.[4] "There is 3 islands" is, of course, a Gallicism; but "much more trees" is a mistake Poles habitually tend to commit. Syntactically flabby sentences, like the one beginning "The looks of the whole establishment . . ." (27 June) sound perfectly normal in Polish, which is a much more inflected and therefore cohesive language.

The diary proper has been used as a source of biographical information and, even more frequently, compared with "Heart of Darkness" for purposes of psychological and factual interpretation of the story. I shall not discuss the parallelisms here, as the ground seems to have been pretty well covered—and also because I am afraid that paying excessive attention to such analogies may be detrimental to a fuller understanding of the story. It may distract us from seeing what it essentially is: not a relation about places and events, but a symbolic presentation of moral and ideological problems. It may also hamper our recognition that Marlow is not the author's mouthpiece, but one of the two main characters of the story, a co-hero, whose point of view is markedly different from the authorial perspective and whose attitudes are even subjected to irony. Generally, the fact that we asume to know much about the personal background of "Heart of Darkness" encourages biographical and psychoanalytic approaches to the tale—which would greatly displease Conrad himself. More important than any autobiographical echoes are the allusions, conscious or not, to literary tradition and, more broadly, to the history of ideas—to the *Aeneid,* to Dante, to the legends about Alexander the Great.[5]

The origins of the two notebooks are different. The "Upriver Book" is written for an obvious and practical purpose: Conrad was expecting to command a steamboat on the Congo and therefore put down data and instructions concerning the best passages, dangerous shallows and snags, wooded places where fuel could be collected, visibility, orientation points, etc. These notes are made from a precise location— the bridge; for a specific purpose—to be used when navigating the boat on the next up-river trip; and for private use— they are in English, although everybody around spoke French. (Conrad served on French ships only as a young apprentice and certainly felt more at ease using English nautical terminology.)

The reasons for keeping the first notebook, the diary proper, are less evident. The practical importance of these jottings is limited: only information concerning distances and directions, and perhaps a few names of people and places, could conceivably be of any future use; these account for only 5 per cent of the text. Most of the remarks have either descriptive or strictly personal content: "Kinzilu rushing in. A short distance from the mouth fine waterfall. Sun rose red— from 9h a.m. infernally hot day. Harou very little better. Self rather seedy. Bathed."

I believe Conrad made these notes with the intention of using them later to refresh his memory. He had by that time written a few chapters of *Almayer's Folly* and was beginning to learn that his imagination must be firmly supported by his own reminiscences—or by studying the reminiscences of others. There are indications that, while on board the *Vidar* (August 1887–January 1888), he also took notes, later used in his Malayan novels.[6] Contrary to Curle's opinion, I think it

is highly probable that the Congo diary was not the only one
Conrad ever kept: after all, we know for certain that he used
to make extensive notes when preparing for and writing his
books.[7] As a beginning author and realizing well the thematic
possibilities offered by his African journey, he apparently
wished to put down some distinct and concrete impressions—
in order to be able later to bolster his memories with hard
data. After arriving at Kinshasa he was, by turn, either too
busy or too sick to continue.

Such a purpose in writing the diary would explain the limitations of its content. Some critics have noted that Conrad's
remarks do not contain any condemnation, any expression of
resentment against atrocities which he must have observed—
if we are to believe "Heart of Darkness"—during his stay in
Matadi and on his walk to Kinshasa. We do not have to as-
sume that the sequence of events in "Heart of Darkness" follows precisely the sequence of Conrad's own experiences. But
anyway, a closer look at the notes shows that—apart from the
first two entries, covering fifteen days and rather bitter in
tone—there are no general statements there, only specific, de-
tailed remarks. For the purpose of future remembering they
were sufficient, and the only pertinent, material.

The descriptions contained in "Heart of Darkness" may
not in particular cases be confirmable either by reference to
Conrad's diary or by other reports; sometimes, when subjected to a piecemeal verification, they may even appear incredible. But the overall picture of the Congo presented by
the story is supported by much contemporary evidence. Thus
a letter, written by an unidentified correspondent just a few
months after Conrad had crossed the same territory and
reporting the impressions of passengers on the same *Roi des
Belges,* strikingly confirms Conrad's assessments: "The country is ruined. Passengers in the steamer *Roi des Belges* have
been able to see for themselves that from Bantja, half a day's
journey below our factory at Upoto, to Bumba inclusive,
there is not an inhabited village left—that is to say four days'
steaming through a country formerly so rich, to-day entirely
ruined."[8]

The first notebook is an obviously interesting document
which acquires even greater biographical value when read in
conjunction with the letters written by Conrad at that time to
Poland and France. Publishing the "Up-river Book" may,

however, need justification. I believe it is worth printing for several reasons. It allows us to witness Conrad at work, using the idiom of his profession—a quite different language from the rather flowery English of his early novels. It reminds us that shapes and colors were the things to which his occupation made him most sensitive. And it provides additional insight into the private factual background of "Heart of Darkness": the importance of securing timber, the feeling of constant tension and insecurity and isolation. The officers on the small (15-ton) steamer were completely preoccupied with navigation and at the same time absolutely cut off from and ignorant of life on the shores of the enormous river.

Curle's statement to the contrary, I think that Conrad did look into his notebooks when writing "Heart of Darkness." Apart from several fragments of the diary proper echoing on pages 70–72,[9] there are two passages which read like excerpts from the "Up-river Book": "I saw an islet, a mere grassy hummock of bright green, in the middle of the stream. It was the only thing of the kind; but as we opened the reach more, I perceived it was the head of a long sandbank, or rather a chain of shallow patches stretching down the middle of the river. . . . I steered her well inshore—the water being deepest near the bank, as the sounding-pole informed me." (p. 108)

Curle is also mistaken in his belief that "we cannot discover where it [the "Up-river Book"] was ended. The last place mentioned is Lulanga." The second part of this notebook is subtitled "from Equator to Bangala" and it is at Bangala—later renamed Nouvelle Anvers—that Conrad stopped writing, on August 19 in the evening.

Why did he interrupt making his notes? There are two possible explanations: one, that he got sick (we know that before the end of the up-river journey he had three attacks of tropical fever);[10] the other, that he either was told or resolved himself that he would not command a vessel on the Congo.

The text published here is based on the original manuscripts of the two Congo notebooks, both now in the Houghton Library, Harvard University. Various brief entries in the first notebook, some of them dating from as late as 1893, which do not form a continuation of the *Congo Diary,* have been left out. J. Miłobędzki, who published the notebooks in a Polish

journal, *Nautologia* (Gdynia, 1972, No. 1 [antedated, in fact
1974]), with a valuable introduction and footnotes, included
some of these scribblings.

Notes

1. G. Jean-Aubry, *Joseph Conrad: Life and Letters,* 2 vols., London, 1926,
vol. I, pp. 141–43.
2. Tadeusz Bobrowski to Conrad, 24 June 1890, Zdzisław Najder, ed.,
Conrad's Polish Background, Oxford University Press, 1964, p. 129.
3. Richard Curle, Introduction to "The Congo Diary," Joseph Conrad,
Last Essays, p. 159. All references to Conrad's works are to the Uniform
Edition, 1923–28.
4. Cf. Arthur P. Coleman, "Polonisms in the English of Conrad's
Chance," Modern Language Notes, XLVI (Nov. 1931), pp. 463–68.
5. On analogies with the *Aeneid* see Lillian Feder, "Marlow's Descent
into Hell," *Nineteenth-century Fiction,* IX (March 1955), pp. 280–92. On
analogies with Virgil and Dante see Robert O. Evans, "Conrad's Under-
world," *Modern Fiction Studies,* II (May 1956), pp. 56–62. Both texts are
reprinted in *The Art of Joseph Conrad: A Critical Symposium,* ed. R. W.
Stallman, Michigan State University Press, 1960.
   The parallel with Alexander the Great has not been so far noticed, although several important elements of the legends about his death resemble
significantly the story of Kurtz. Alexander demanded to be paid the homage
due to a god, and killed Callisthenes, who refused to do so. When he fell ill
with malaria, he had himself carried on a litter to attend sacrifices. His soldiers thronged to see him and pay him tribute. Although greatly weakened,
he wanted to be honored and deluded himself about his recovery. The night
before he died, he crawled out on all fours from his palace to drown himself
in the Euphrates, hoping that his body would be lost and people would believe that he had disappeared like an immortal god. But his wife traced him
and brought him back to die in bed. Kurtz is also the object of a cult, takes
part in human sacrifices, falls ill with fever, accepts last tributes when
carried on a stretcher, tries to escape—on all fours—back to his worshipers,
is captured and dies in bed; etc., etc.
6. Jocelyn Baines, *Joseph Conrad: A Critical Biography,* London, 1960,
p. 90.
7. E.g., the notes discovered by Norman Sherry (Times Literary Supple-
ment, 25 June 1970). Conrad frequently mentions making notes for
planned novels in his letters to his literary agent, James B. Pinker.
8. Quoted in Edmond D. Morel, *Red Rubber,* Manchester–London, 1906,
p. 40.
9. Joseph Conrad, *Youth and Two Other Stories* (Uniform Edition).
10. Conrad to Marguerite Poradowska, 26 September 1890, *Letters of
Joseph Conrad to Marguerite Poradowska, 1890–1920,* ed. John A. Gee
and Paul J. Sturm, Yale University Press, 1940, p. 16.

The Congo Diary

Arrived at Matadi on the 13th of June, 1890.[1]

Mr. Gosse, chief of the station (O.K.) retaining us for some reason of his own.[2]

Made the acquaintance of Mr. Roger Casement,[3] which I should consider as a great pleasure under any circumstances and now it becomes a positive piece of luck.

Thinks, speaks well, most intelligent and very sympathetic.

Feel considerably in doubt about the future. Think just now that my life amongst the people (white) around here cannot be very comfortable. Intend avoid acquaintances as much as possible.

Through Mr. R.C. have made the acquain[tan]ce of Mr. Underwood, the Manager of the English Factory (Hatton & Cookson) in Kalla Kalla. Av[era]ge com[merci]al hearty and kind. Lunched there on the 21st.

24th. Gosse and R.C. gone with a large lot of ivory down to Boma. On G.['s] return to start to up the river. Have been myself busy packing ivory in casks. Idiotic employment. Health good up to now.

Wrote to Simpson,[4] to Gov. B.,[5] to Purd.,[6] to Hope,[7] to Capt. Froud,[8] and to Mar.[9] Prominent characteristic of the social life here: people speaking ill of each other.

Saturday, 28th June. Left Matadi with Mr. Harou[10] and a caravan of 31 men. Parted with Casement in a very friendly manner. Mr. Gosse saw us off as far as the State station.

First halt, M'poso. 2 Danes in Comp[a]ny.[11]

Sund[ay], 29th. Ascent of Pataballa sufficiently fatiguing. Camped at 11h a.m. at Nsoke River. Mosquitos.[12]

Monday, 30th. To Congo da Lemba after passing black rocks long ascent. Harou giving up. Bother. Camp bad. Water far. Dirty. At night Harou better.

Tuesday, 1st. Left early in a heavy mist, marching towards Lufu River. Part route through forest on the sharp slope of a high mountain. Very long descent. Then market place from where short walk to the bridge (good) and camp. V.[ery] G.[ood] Bath. Clear river. Feel well. Harou all right. 1st chicken, 2 p.[m.]. No sunshine today.

Wednesday, 2nd July.

Started at 5:30 after a sleepless night. Country more open. Gently andulating[13] hill. Road good in perfect order. (District of Lukungu.)

Feel not well today. Heavy cold in the head. Arrived at 11 at Banza Manteka. Camped on the market place. Not well enough to call on the missionary. Water scarce and bad. Camp[in]g place dirty. 2 Danes still in Company.

Thursday, 3rd July.

Left at 6 a.m. after a good night's rest. Crossed a low range of hills and entered a broad valley, or rather plain with a break in the middle. Met an off[ic]er of the State inspecting; a few minutes afterwards saw at a camp[in]g place the dead body of a Backongo. Shot? Horrid smell. Crossed a range of mountains, running NW–SE by a low pass. Another broad flat valley with a deep ravine through the centre. Clay and gravel. Another range parallel to the first mentioned, with a chain of low foothills running close to it. Between the two came to camp on the banks of the Luinzono River. Camp[in]g place clean. River clear Gov[ernmen]t Zanzibari[14] with register. Canoe. 2 danes camp[in]g on the other bank. Health good.

General tone of landscape gray-yellowish (dry grass), with reddish patches (soil) and clumps of dark-green vegetation scattered sparsely about, mostly in steep gorges between the high mountains or in ravines cutting the plain. Noticed Palma Christi— Oil palm. Very straight, tall and thick trees in some places. Name not known to me. Villages quite invisible. Infer their existence from cal[a]bashes suspended to palm trees for the "malafu." Good many caravans and travellers. No women unless on the market place.

Bird notes charming. One especially, a flute-like note. Another kind of "boom" ressembling[15] the very distant baying of a hound. Saw only pigeons and a few green parroquets; very small and not many. No birds of prey seen by me. Up to 9 a.m. sky clouded and calm. Afterwards gentle breeze from the N[or]th generally and sky clearing. Nights damp and cool. White mists on the hills up about halfway. Water effects very beautiful this morning. Mists generally raising before sky clears.

Section of today's road.

[a drawing: section of the day's march]

General direction NNE–SSW

Distance—15 miles.

Friday, 4th July.

Left camp at 6h a.m. after a very unpleasant night. Marching across a chain of hills and then in a maze of hills. At 8:15 opened out into an andulating plain. Took bearings of a break in the chain of mountains on the other side. Bearing NNE. Road passes through that. Sharp ascents up very steep hills not very high. The higher mountains recede sharply and show a low hilly country. At 9:30 market place.

At 10h passed R. Lukanga and at 10:30 camped on the Mpwe R.

Today's march. Direction NNE½N. Dist[an]ce 13 miles.

[section of the day's march]

Saw another dead body lying by the path in an attitude of meditative repose.

In the evening three women of whom[16] one albino passed our camp. Horrid chalky white with pink blotches. Red eyes. Red hair. Features very Negroid and ugly. Mosquitos. At night when the moon rose heard shouts and drumming in distant villages. Passed a bad night.

Saturday, 5th July. go.

Left at 6:15. Morning cool, even cold and very damp. Sky densely overcast. Gentle breeze from NE. Road through a narrow plain up to R. Kwilu. Swift-flowing and deep, 50 yds. wide. Passed in canoes. After[war]ds up and down very steep hills intersected by deep ravines. Main chain of heights running mostly

NW–SE or W and E at times. Stopped at Manyamba. Camp[in]g
place bad—in hollow—water very indifferent. Tent set at 10:15.
Section of today's road. NNE Distance 12 m.
[a drawing]
Today fell into a muddy puddle. Beastly. The fault of the man
that carried me. After camp[in]g went to a small stream, bathed
and washed clothes. Getting jolly well sick of this fun.
Tomorrow expect a long march to get to Nsona, 2 days from
Manyanga. No sunshine today.

Sunday, 6th July.
Started at 5:40. The route at first hilly, then after a sharp de-
scent traversing a broad plain. At the end of it a large market
place. At 10h sun came out.
After leaving the market, passed another plain, then walking on
the crest of a chain of hills passed 2 villages and at 11h arrived at
Nsona. Village invisible.
Section of day's march.
[a drawing]
Direction about NNE.
Distance—18 miles.
In this camp (Nsona) there is a good camp[in]g place. Shady.
Water far and not very good. This night no mosquitos owing to
large fires lit all round our tent.
Afternoon very close. Night clear and starry.

Monday, 7th July.
Left at 6h after a good night's rest on the road to Inkandu,
which is some distance past Lukungu Gov[ernmen]t station.
Route very accidented.[17] Succession of round steep hills. At
times walking along the crest of a chain of hills.
Just before Lukunga our carriers took a wide sweep to the
southward till the station bore N[or]th. Walking through long
grass for 1½ hours. Crossed a broad river about 100 feet wide
and 4 deep. After another ½ hour's walk through manioc planta-
tions in good order, rejoined our route to the Ed[18] of the Lukunga
Sta[ti]on. Walking along an andulating plain towards the Inkandu
market on a hill. Hot, thirsty and tired. At 11h arrived in the
M[ar]ket place. About 200 people. Business brisk. No water. No

camp[in]g place. After remaining for one hour, left in search of a resting place.

Row with carriers. No water. At last, about 1½ p.m., camped on an exposed hillside near a muddy creek. No shade. Tent on a slope. Sun heavy. Wretched.

[section of the day's march]

Direction NE by N.

Distance—22 miles.

Night miserably cold. No sleep. Mosquitos.

Tuesday, 8th July.

Left at 6h a.m.

About ten minutes from camp left main gov[ernmen]t path for the Manyanga track. Sky overcast. Road up and down all the time. Passing a couple of villages.

The country presents a confused wilderness of hills land slips on their sides showing red. Fine effect of red hill covered in places by dark-green vegetation.

½ hour before beginning the descent got a glimpse of the Congo. Sky clouded.

Today's march—3h.

[section of the day's march]

General direction N by E.

Dist[an]ce 9½ miles.

Arrived at Manyanga at 9h a.m.

Received most kindly by Messrs. Heyn[19] & Jaeger. Most comfortable and pleasant halt.

Stayed here till the 25th.[20] Both have been sick. Most kindly care taken of us. Leave with sincere regret.

			(Mafiesa)
Fridy 25th	Nkenghe		LEFT
Sat. 26	Nsona		Nkendo
Sun. 27	Nkandu		LUASI
Mon. 28	Nkonzo		(Nkoma)
Tue. 29	Nkenghe		Nzungi
Wed. 30	Nsona		Inkissi
Thur. 31	Nkandu	mercredi	Stream
Fri. 1 Aug.	Nkonzo		Luila

Sat. 2   Nkenghe   Nselenba
Sun. 3   Nsona
Mon. 4   Nkandu
Tue. 5   Nkonzo
Wed. 6   Nkenghe[21]

Friday, the 25th July, 1890.
    Left Manyanga at 2½ p.m. with plenty of hammock carriers. H.
lame and not in very good form. Myself ditto but not lame.
Walked as far as Mafiela and camped—2h.

Saturday, 26th.
    Left very early. Road ascending all the time. Passed villages.
Country seems thickly inhabited. At 11h arrived at large market
place. Left at noon and camped at 1h p.m.
[section of the day's march with notes]
a camp—a white man died here—market—govt. post—mount—
crocodile pond—Mafiesa
    Gen. direction E½N—W½S.
    Sun visible at 8 am. Very hot. Distance—18 miles.

Sunday, 27th.
    Left at 8h am. Sent luggage carriers straight on to Luasi and
went ourselves round by the Mission of Sutili.
    Hospitable reception by Mrs. Comber. All the missio[naries]
absent.
    The looks of the whole establishment eminently civilized and
very refreshing to see after the lots of tumble-down hovels in
which the State and Company agents are content to live—fine
buildings. Position on a hill. Rather breezy.
    Left at 3h pm. At the first heavy ascent met Mr. Davis,
miss[ionary] returning from a preaching trip. Rev. Bentley[22] away
in the South with his wife.
    This being off the road, no section given. Distance traversed
about 15 miles. General direction ENE.
    At Luasi we get on again on to the Gov[ernmen]t road.
    Camped at 4½ pm. With Mr. Heche in company.
    Today no sunshine.
    Wind remarkably cold. Gloomy day.

Monday, 28th.

Left camp at 6:30 after breakfasting with Heche.

Road at first hilly. Then walking along the ridges of hill chains with valleys on both sides. The country more open and there is much more trees[23] growing in large clumps in the ravines.

Passed Nzungi and camped 11h on the right bank of Ngoma, a rapid little river with rocky bed. Village on a hill to the right.

[section of the day's march]

General direction ENE.

Distance—14 miles.

No sunshine. Gloomy cold day. Squalls.

Tuesday, 29th.

Left camp at 7h after a good night's rest. Continuous ascent; rather easy at first. Crossed wooded ravines and the river Lunzadi by a very decent bridge.

At 9h met Mr. Louette escorting a sick agent of the Comp[an]y back to Matadi. Looking very well. Bad news from up the river. All the steamers disabled. One wrecked.[24] Country wooded. At 10:30 camped at Inkissi.

[section of the day's march]

General direction ENE.

Dist[an]ce—15 miles.

Sun visible at 6:30. Very warm day.

Inkissi River very rapid, is about 100 yards broad. Passage in canoes. Banks wooded very densely and valley of the river rather deep but very narrow.

Today did not set the tent but put up in Gov[ernmen]t shimbek.[25] Zanzibari in charge—very obliging. Met ripe pineapple for the first time. On the road today passed a skeleton tied up to a post. Also white man's grave—no name. Heap of stones in the form of a cross.

Health good now.

Wednesday, 30th.

Left at 6 a.m. intending to camp at Kinfumu. Two hours' sharp walk brought me to Nsona na Nsefe. Market. ½ hour after, Harou arrived very ill with billious [sic] attack and fever. Laid

him down in Gov[ernmen]t shimbek. Dose of Ipeca.[26] Vomiting
bile in enormous quantities. At 11h gave him 1 gramme of qui-
nine and lots of hot tea. Hot fit ending in heavy perspiration. At 2
p.m. put him in hammock and started for Kinfumu. Row with carriers all the way. Harou suffering much through the jerks of the
hammock. Camped at a small stream.

At 4h Harou better. Fever gone.

[section of the day's march with notes]

wooded—camp—grass—Nsona a Nsefe—wood stream—open—
wood—Lulufu River—a remarkable conical mountain bearing
NE visible from here—Inkissi.

General direction NE by E.

Distance—13 miles.

Up till noon, sky clouded and strong NW wind very chilling.
From 1h pm to 4h pm sky clear and very hot day. Expect lots
of bother with carriers tomorrow. Had them all called and made a
speech which they did not understand. They promise good behav-
iour.

Thursday, 31st.

Left at 6h. Sent Harou ahead and followed in ½ an hour. Road
presents several sharp ascents and a few others easier but rather
long. Notice in places sandy surface soil instead of hard clay as
heretofore; think, however, that the layer of sand is not very thick
and that the clay would be found under it. Great difficulty in car-
rying Harou. Too heavy. Bother. Made two long halts to rest the
carriers. Country wooded in valleys and on many of the ridges.

Section of today's road.

[a drawing]

At 2:30 pm reached Luila at last and camped on right bank.
Breeze from SW.

General direction of march about NE½E.

Distance est[imated]—16 miles.

Congo very narrow and rapid. Kinzilu rushing in. A short distance up from the mouth fine waterfall.

Sun rose red—from 9h a.m. Infernally hot day.

Harou very little better.

Self rather seedy. Bathed. Luila about 60 feet wide. Shallow.

Friday, 1st of August 1890.

Left at 6:30 am after a very indifferently passed night. Cold, heavy mists. Road in long ascents and sharp dips all the way to Mfumu Mbé.

After leaving there, a long and painful climb up a very steep hill; then a long descent to Mfumu Kono where a long halt was made. Left at 12:30 p.m. towards Nselemba. Many ascents. The aspect of the country entirely changed. Wooded hills with openings. Path almost all the afternoon thro' a forest of light trees with dense undergrowth.

After a halt on a wooded hillside reached Nselemba at 4h 10 m p.m.

[section of the day's march]

Put up at Gov[ernmen]t shanty.

Row between the carriers and a man stating himself in Gov[ernmen]t employ, about a mat. Blows with sticks raining hard. Stopped it. Chief came with a youth about 13 suffering from gunshot wound in the head. Bullet entered about an inch above the right eyebrow and came out a little inside. The roots of the hair, fairly in the middle of the brow in a line with the bridge of the nose. Bone not damaged apparently. Gave him a little glycerine to put on the wound made by the bullet on coming out. Harou not very well. Mosquitos. Frogs. Beastly. Glad to see the end of this stupid tramp. Feel rather seedy. Sun rose red. Very hot day. Wind S[ou]th.

General direction of march—NE by N.
Distance—about 17 miles.

Notes to The Congo Diary

1. An important colonial station about forty miles up from Boma at the mouth of the Congo. Conrad arrived there by boat, on his way to take up the command of a river steamship in Kinshasa.
2. The recently nominated director of Matadi station of the Société Anonyme pour le Commerce du Haut-Congo.
3. This future Irish nationalist leader (1864–1916) was at the time employed by the Société as supervisor of a planned railway, connecting Matadi with Kinshasa. He had been to the Congo before, in 1887. Later he became

British Vice-Consul for the Congo and in 1903 prepared a widely publicized report on atrocities committed by Belgian colonialists.

4. James H. Simpson, of the Australian shipowning firm Henry Simpson & Sons, to which the barque *Otago* belonged, commanded by Conrad between January 1888 and March 1889 (his only command).

5. Tadeusz Bobrowski (1829–94), his maternal uncle and guardian.

6. R. Curle suggests that it was "captain Purdy, an acquaintance of Conrad" (*Last Essays*, p. 161). Nothing, however, is known about this person. William Purdu of Glasgow served, as first mate, together with Conrad on *Loch Etive* in 1880. (J. Allen, *The Sea Years of Joseph Conrad*, New York, 1965, p. 318.)

7. George Fountaine Weare Hope, Conrad's friend in London, businessman and ex-seaman.

8. The Secretary of London Ship-Master Society.

9. Marguerite Poradowska (1848–1937), widow of his cousin Aleksander Poradowski. She helped Conrad in obtaining his position in the Congo. The letter is dated June 18.

10. Prosper Harou, an agent of the Société, who arrived from Europe on the same boat as Conrad.

11. Many Scandinavians served as officers on the Society's steamboats. Cf. N. Sherry, *Conrad's Western World*, Cambridge, 1971, pp. 17–91.

12. Always spelled thus in the diary.

13. Several times spelled so in the diary. The beginning "u" in "undulating" is pronounced like the Polish "a."

14. The Congo Free State frequently employed Zanzibaris as soldiers or policemen.

15. After the French *ressemblant*.

16. "Which" crossed out.

17. From the French *accidenté*—uneven, rough, hilly.

18. Mistake for "East."

19. The new chief of the Society's station at Manyanga.

20. Conrad never fully explained the reasons for this protracted stay.

21. A list of personal carriers or chief carriers on duty. In the right column names of places passed. A similar list, in French, giving the order of duty for the period 28 June–9 July, is found at the end of the diary.

22. Rev. W. Holman Bentley, author of *Pioneering in the Congo*, London, 1900.

23. From the Polish *wiele więcej drzew*.

24. The *Florida* was wrecked on July 18, but was refloated and brought back to Kinshasa in five days. (N. Sherry, p. 41.)

25. Word differently spelled in various African languages and dialects; a few huts occupied by people of the same employment (e.g., railway builders).

26. Ipecacuanha, an herb medicine against dysentery.

Up-river Book
Commenced 3. Aug[u]st 1890
S.S. "Roi des Belges"

On leaving—from A after passing the two islands steer for clump—high tree. two isl[and]
points. Sandy beach.

[Two sketches with contours of land and islands,
marked: N°I, A, trees, sandy, point, bay, foul,
and stones]

N°II Steer for inside sandy point, then keep
out (about East by the sun). As you approach
coast breaks out into islands—B Steer for end
marked B. *From position C. a further point visible.* C. Steer for sandbank II, behind hazy
clumps of trees visible on a point of land. No is-

N°III.IV.

lands visible. Left bank island presents appearance of mainland. Bank II covered at H[igh]
W[ater]. Come up right to the bank I. Pass near
islet y. Leave bank II on on port side. Steer for
sandy path on S[ou]th shore.

Position D. Point *a* looks low now. S[ou]th
side sandbank cov[ered] at H[igh] W[ater].

The opening narrows. Point *a* advancing.

Position E.

Low land and outlying sandbanks a little to
port. Steering for a little square white patch.
Stick on it. Pass close to the sands—*Cautiously!*

N°V. (and also IV)

Position F. ENE. Patch about ESE—Pass
along sand shore not far from point △ steering
well in. Island X on the starboard side and gen-

erally kept ahead. On the port side (left bank) extensive and dangerous sand bank. 1½ foot (*Capt Coch*)[1] As you proceed in point ⊙ seems closed in with island X and apparently no passage. Further on it opens again. A small grassy patch marks the end of point ⊙ High hills right ahead looming behind island X.

Come right up to the island, then steer along shore to the point ⊙ a little on the port bow as from *position F.a.* Coming up to a white patch after opening a small channel cutting X in two. A small island app[arent]ly closes the passage. When nearing the end of X *must* keep close and steer into the bay 8 getting the clump of trees on the port side. Going out the highest mountain will be right ahead—always keep the high mountain ahead crossing over to the left bank. To port of highest mount a low black point. Opposite a long island stretching across. The shore is wooded.

V.Va.

As you approach the shore the black point and the island close in together—No danger. Steering close to the mainland between the island and the grassy sandbank, towards the high mount[ain]s steering close to the left bank *of the river all the time. Entered.*

VI. On left bank wooded point.

Right valley. 1st Reach nearly north.

2nd Reach about NNE.

Left bank. Wooded point.

3d Reach the same and wooded point.

4th Reach NbyE.

Point III. Stones off.

IV. Before getting abreast there is a rocky shoal ⅓ out. 9 hours after entering the river sighted "2 sago-trees point" not at all remarkable. Low flat at the foot of the hills. The appearance of point VI is bushy. Rather low. Round slope behind as per sketch.

Just before coming up to p[oin]t VI got bottom at 6 feet stones. Hauled out. Point VII called "Sandstone Pt." with a small ledge of rock outside of it.

Before closing with it cross over to the right bank.

Moored to—grassy Beach backed by trees. 25 Miles from the entrance—5ʰ30.

4th Aug. VII This reach is about *E.* Shortly after leaving, point A opens out double in peculiar shape. Off point VIII long stone ridge. Point A has a small sand-spit covered at full river. Right below the point there is a small sandbank along the shore. Wooding place. May get in between sandbank and the shore. After passing A point in the middle of the river there is a rocky ledge now above water. Covered at F[ull] W[ater]. River rather narrow. Steering well off the right bank.

Snake tree point has a ledge of rock lying well off. To give a wide berth.

Here begins a reach about NE (by the sun). On the left bank many palms visible.

After passing Sn[ake] Tree point on the left bank entrance to Black River—A remark[ab]le clump little further on *R. bank—Point C.*

Off point C. *cross over.* On the left bank on point XI one palm rather conspicuous when coming up. After turning point C. you open up a remarkable point running from high mountains called point Licha. Wooding place. (6h am.) On the right bank past point C. sandy beaches to be met often. On left bank a little past XI point there is a market place. Rocky shoals near in shore.

From Licha point up. VIII

From Licha—crossing over to right bank where there is outcrop of rock. Small sandy beach near.   *Left 6:15*

Bearing Licha	S15°W	)	Time
Point C	S25°W	)	6:35
Point XII.	N48°E	)	h.m.
Point D.	N34°E	)	6:35/
Point F	N36°E		7:15

Rate about 3½ miles per *h*

After leaving Licha keep in the middle

G. N33°E   9ʰ20ᵐ   bearing from p[oin]t XII.

Pt XIII   8:15   opposite XII rocky cliff with

Pt XIV from   ledges extending

p[o]s[itio]n   After point XII indented shore with a low

b[earing]   shore with a low flat

NEbyN½[N]   running at the foot of the

                          hills. After passing XIII

                          rocky sweep—this reach

                          is NEbyN.—Steer by the left bank

                          2 low points with many

Point H   palms in the bight.

at 10ʰ50ᵐ   An island in the middle

                          of the bight.

                          Before closing with G

                          point small S[and] B[ank] parallel

                          to the shore—pass[age] inside(?)

IX

Pt XV bore   ⎫   good wooding place.

NEbyN½N   ⎪   After passing 1ˢᵗ island open up a point and

from x pᵗ   ⎬   sight a long and a very small island. Island No.

Pᵗ K bore   ⎪   2 long wooded. Small islet No. 3—This reach is

NNE from   ⎬   NEbyN nearly.

Isᵈ 3   ⎭   Between Is[lan]d No. 2 and No. 3 rocky

Islet N 3   ledges and no passage. From abreast P[oin]t H

at 10ʰ50ᵐ   it seems as if Is. 3 was abreast Point XIV. The

                          NW End of Is[lan]d 2 has a palm grove—The

                          island lays NW–SE.

                          All along right shore small beaches—and dead

                          wood on most of them. After passing point

                          XIV a long stretch of low land on left bank

                          with islands (very small). A remarkable clump

Island N 4   of trees as per chart and many palm trees on

at Noon.   the low shore.

Island No 4   This stretch of low land continues for a long

   to   time with many palms.

Point M   General appearance light green.

NEbyE   Long reach with a regular sweep on the left

2ʰ30ᵐ p.m.   bank from Island No. 4 2½ up.

                             X. This Reach is *NEbyN*. Directly after passing p[oin]t M. on the right shore rocky shoals extending good way out.

Afterwards same appearance. Hills to water's edge with small sandy beaches.

Over p[oin]t XVI curious yellow path on a hill.

Steering a little over on the right bank side. On the other side villages on slope of hill. After point N another p[oin]t forming a high plain.

At N
3ʰ45ᵐ

A little further ridge of rocks. Before coming to high plain p[oin]t N° 2 is a wooding place. P[oin]t bore NEbyN at 4ʰ25ᵐ from high plain P[oin]t N°2. Abreast point XVII at 5ʰ10ᵐ/length of reach 5½ m. The new reach about NE½N. Abreast point XVII a long parallel ridge of rocks well off the shore.

Off Point P a long rocky ridge extending into the river (from here in one day to Kichassa down stream. 12 hours steaming).

All the time keeping over to the French shore.

Hills on left shore present a reddish appearance. All the right bank fringed with trees. At the small beach near Point P at 5ʰ50ᵐ—moored —Wooding places—Villages on the opposite bank.

Point P. 6ʰ0ᵐ
End of point
Bankap bore
NEbyN from mid[d]le
of the river.
A little past
Pᵗ P.
7ʰ45 at point
XVIII

Left. Cross over from the beach below the Point P.

Here commences a reach about *NE*.

After rounding P[oin]t P. there is a wooding place. Narrow beach.

From there steer a little over where there is a small island not app[aren]t. No passage. After that keep nearly in the middle.

All that shore is a low flat fringed by trees backed by low hills. Bordered by reefs.

Steer in the middle—till abreast p[oin]t Q. then a little over to the right bank—

XI After p[oin]t XVIII a [sic] invisible sandbank stretches along the right shore. Keep off nearly in center.

from Camp
to
XVIII–6 miles
16¾

Bankab–NEbyN

Pt XVIII at *7ʰ45ᵐ*
times
from XVIII
Reach—NEbyN½N.
to pt R.
at 9ʰam
from XVIII to
R. 1ʰ45ᵐ or
say 6 miles.
NEbyN ½N.
Bankab Pt
9ʰ15ᵐ
Ganchu bore
N½W

Point R from mi[d]dle NNE. On pt Bankab two
high trees—one broad another less spreading.

About 1 hour after passing pt XVIII—passing
the wooded false points rocks extend out into the
river. P[oin]t Q bearing about N[or]th and Bankab about NNE.

On nearing p[oin]t Bankab on French shore to
the N[or]th [of] p[oin]t Q small island/N°6/and
long sandbank over which from the middle of
the river you see Ganchu P[oin]t bearing about
NbyE. The islet N°6 has a few trees and a dead
palm on it. Opp[osi]te on same shore in a ravine
small vill[ag]e. Round Bank[ab] in back cur-
r[ent].

When rounding Bankab keep on Right side
and enter the current sweeping out of the bight
cautiously and end on nearly.

(On coming down follow the current round
the bight.)

When about the middle of the open snatch
steer right across to clear Ganchu's Point. Pass
the point cautiously. Stones. Then steer straight
for P[oin]t XIX. Along the left shore below the
point stretches of a sandbank ressembling a
beach but covered at F[ull] W[ater].

Pt XIX at
10ʰ40ᵐ
Pt S bore N.

From p[oin]t XIX cross over a little of a small
beach on the opposite side by compass about
NbyW½W.

This short Reach is about *NNE*. Next short
Reach is about NEbyN½N

Keeping a little over on the right shore. On
the left bank bushes growing down to the water.
Right shore low, undulating. Wooded (Coming
down from S the false XIX point should be
alone visible).

Pt.S. *at Noon* 12ʰ.

Pt XX bore N½E.

Entrance of River Kassai. NEbyN.

Point on right bank white patch bore N½W.

Next pt to S. N¾W.

XII. Entrance to Kassai rather broad. On
S[ou]th side a bright beach with a spreading
dead tree above it mark the mouth.

At the Cath[oli]c mission moor alongside the head of the beach.

From P[oin]t S to Mission. NNE.1ʰ

Made fast at 1ʰ p.m.

Pt XX. bore N5°W

Left the mission at 2½—In the bight between the miss[ion] and P[oin]t XX rocky ledges. Off P[oin]t XX a stony ridge partially cover[e]d at high water.

From XX.
Pt T.
bore
NbyE½E
at 3ʰ20ᵐ
p.m.

Off Pt XX at 3ʰ20ᵐ making it about 2ʰ from the Pt S.

After passing P[oin]t XX follow the left shore at some distance to the p[oin]t with the grassy slope about NNE. From there cross over towards point T. Sandbank always covered in the bight. Current easy in the middle.

Off
Point T
at 5ʰ25
Point XXI bore
N¾E

Probably there is a passage between the sand and the left bank.

This reach about N. (Stopped at 5ʰ45ᵐ.)

Left stopping place at 7ʰ am.

On Right bank—from stopping place sighted a dark-green p[oin]t—a long spit of sand cov[ere]d at full water with high rocks also cov[ere]d at very full water.

On *left shore* a sandb[an]k always covered extends ⅓ᵈ into the river.

Got soundings below the dark-green P[oin]t bearing NbyWest. P[oin]t XXI bore NEbyE. *3 fth and 4 fth*²

[Proceeding up you open the Lawson River Entrance]³ Opening Lawson River with sandbank across the mouth and rocks stretching off. Further a long cut beach. P[oin]t XXI gets indistinct on nearer approach. No danger on that side.

XIII

A small rocky ledge on the point Past Pt XXI at⁴ This reach about NbyE. After passing

P[oin]t XXI—R[i]g[h]t bank low scrubby and
trees. Sm[all] hills. To the left higher hills with
bare tops and a belt of forest halfway up from
the water's edge At P[oin]t U—Wooding places.
Caution The landing must be approached cautiously on account of stones and snags. Round
P[oin]t U cautiously. When entering the reach
keep rather on the outer edge of the current following the right shore. Sandbank on left shore
not visible.

From 3 fath[oms] position the P[oin]t XXII
bears NEbyE. The middle of uncovered S[outh]
B[an]k bears about N½E.

A spit with 1½ fth at less than ½ full river
extends towards U high land. On rounding
P[oin]t XXII give a wide berth. There is [sic] 2
stony ledges of which the outer one is cov[ere]d
at full river. This reach about NEbyN. Before
passing Mission P[oin]t you open out false
p[oin]t W which is not noticeable. Also a point
on the left shore. Coast in perfect semicircle
sand, swamp and trees—hills opened out there.
A few high thin trees dispersed in that stretch.

As you near the end of the semicircle the
M[ission] marked in sketch disappears.

From the same place Island N 7 bore N¾E.—
from point (Eng[lish] Mission)[5] at Grenfell
p[oin]t—at *4ʰ* p.m.

When passing the dangerous sandbank called
mission sands keep close in with M[issi]on Point
and have the island either on port bow or starboard quarter till you clear M[issi]on Point.

[A sketch with contours of shore, islands, a
sandbank and the ship's track represented by a
dotted line etc. Islands (or parts of the mainland) numbered: 8, 9 and 10. A point on No. 10
marked B.]

NE   EbyN   NEbyE   NE
Square little beach ahead △
and bore Sth   NNW   Nth
    From Pt B.   *Island 11*

careful of

snags opposite the dead tree

Passage inside island 10 at full water.

Passage inside small islet off 2 Palm P[oin]t at full water. When must keep close inshore keep close to Island 12—over a bank with 2 fath. After passing Is[lan]d 12 steer for bush on end of the long island.

Koch's passage

From there for bush point on the M[ai]n land follow cut bank, then cross over towards low island.

XIV

Sandbank right across after approaching in— steer along it towards the tree on it and pass between it and the M[ai]nland (when nearing 1 fth. to 1½ fth.).

Steer in middle of passage and then for XXIV p[oin]t following the bight of the shore. From p[oin]t XXIV steer between two small islands keeping over to starboard. Soundings in 1, 1½, 1 fath—variable. Bolobo village. Landing place. A few minutes after passing the mission keep out a little into the river.

This reach from the mission is about NE. Follow the right bank, the courses being from NE till you open the bend of low shore. Then P[oin]t of M[ai]nland bearing NEbyE and small island bearing EbyNth.

Steer in the bend a little watching for edge of sandbank. Leave the small island on St[arboar]d side. Sandbanks on both sides with spits across the course. After nearing island 12 another small island is seen to be left to starb[oar]d. General direction of land from there is ENE. After passing the island keep at mod[era]te distance off.

XV

When app[roa]ch[in]g long islands there is a bank with 1 fth at ½ full. Close in a little with the main.

After passing steep round bank steer in with the bend. When off the swamp spit all the islands on the southern bearing seem one land.

XVa

Arrived at stopping place at 5ʰ30ᵐ. Village.

Left stopping place at 6 am. Steering for

P[oin]t XXV keep in with the bend. Remarkable. Islands.

XVI   Island bearing NE. Square clump light green. Follow the island *15th* shore all the time— remarkable palm—second small island, then steer for little grassy islet.

Soundings in 1½ and 1 fth. Course about ENE. Leave grassy islet on St[arboar]d hand and steer in 1½ to 2 fth for island bearing ENE N° 16.

XVII   Follow the shore of island N° 16 on an *NE½E* course. *Mind the snags* along island N° 16.

Cross over well before getting to Pool P[oin]t.

Cross to where higher trees begin.

When nearing M[ai]nland p[oin]t you will see the open passage between Is[lan]d 17 and 18.

XVIII   The entrance to the Oubangi is barred on the up-river side by extensive sandbanks. The opposite Congo shore forms a ½ circle from the F[ren]ch mission[6] to P[oin]t XXVI.

When rounding P[oin]t XXVI the current is very strong. Rocks off the p[oin]t. Sandbank stretching close from the N[or]th towards it always covered but impassable at any state of the river. Inside the bight steer close in to guard against dangerous snags. Rounding the points pretty close you sight to port the commencement of a long island called Flat Is[lan]d. Proceeding on pass the village of Pressinbi then Irebu.

Sharp bend in the shore where the mouth of the R[iver Oubangui] is. From elbow cross over to the flat island avoiding S[and]b[an]ks and snags—then where a few palms form clump cross over again and follow main shore.

Rounding another point still follow main shore at times only 2 to 1½ fath[oms] water. Otherwise passage not intricate. Otherwise keep generally by the line indicated on the chart.

After leaving Irebu there is no wooding place for some time.

XXIII. and A. Thursday—14th Aug[u]st. Left stopping place at 6.10ᵐ.

Pass outside the sm[all] islet in the first bend after leaving. The general direction since yesterday[7]

Entering the next narrow reach keep on but at a little dist[an]ce from left shore—Snags—This reach is safe across (Koch). A succession of canal-like bends. The shore covered with dense forest right down to water's edge.

The river opens suddenly disclosing more islands.

XXIV After rounding the last P[oin]t of the narrow part the channel lies SE. Then ahead you have 3 islands looking at first like one. As you near the point opposite them they open out. Off that point sandbank runs over to the islands—go over it. XXV.

Then a wide bight of the main shore is entered. On the P[or]t side many islands presenting varied aspects from different places. The general direction is NE½N about.

Keep pretty well on the main shore watching for snags all along.

On the port side extensive sandbanks partly visible but mostly covered at ½ F[ull] W[ater]. Both shores heavily timbered with dense undergrowth. After sighting a long island and following it for some time you enter a NbyE reach, then you enter a narrow passage between two islands NEbyE. At the end of short passage islands in sight again and the river broadens out. A broad stretch where the course is about NE½E. All islands seen from the broad passage are now shut together into one. XXVI

Entering another broad expansion of the river follow cautiously the courses set on the chart XXVI V[i]ll[a]ge of Ikongo—Bad. XXVII Rounding the next 2 points there is another broad stretch comparatively free of sandb[an]ks. Steer from p[oin]t to p[oin]t on the main shore having always the islands on your p[or]t hand. General direction about *NE.*

Main shore less thickly overgrown now— Islands all heavily timbered. After passing

XVII

Lower Mission Point a small bay *with* stones in
it. Beaches coloured *red*. After passing 2 more
points you sight the Am[erican] Mission[8] in the
bottom of a small bight. Hardly vis[i]ble. A big
dead tree marks it exactly.

II Part
in N[or]th Lat[itu]de from Equator to Bangala

*Charts in Nth Lat^{de} Saturday—16th Aug^{st},
1890–7^h30^m*

Left Equator—Follow the bank. Short distance
round the first point pass State Station.

River narrowed by islands. App[arent]ly no
sandbanks. After passing the 2^d point the next
reach broadens out. Courses: NNE–NE and
ENE.

After passing a point with tall trees you open
out a reach about E.

A low point of land without trees bearing east
marks the appr[oa]ch of Berouki R[iver][9]

The other bank of the Berouki is covered with
forest growth, Two sm[all] islands mark the entrance of the south arm of the delta. Steering
about NE close to two small islands to port of
you you app[roa]ch the point of the second arm
of the Berouki delta.

Steer close to it pass[in]g over 3 fth., the next
reach being NbyW very nearly.

Soon another branch of the delta is passed.
Very narrow.

The NbyW reach ends at a low point after
pass[in]g a sm[all] clearing and a one-limbed
tree. Pass small river II N. The next reach opens
on about the same width, two small islands
forming the bend. Direction N[or]th.

River perhaps a little wider in this reach—The
same appearance of the banks. Dense growth of
bushes and not very tall trees of a dark green
tint. On the port side S[and]b[ank] visible before
reach. Point. After passing the point a straight
reach due North, not very long. ⅔^{ds} up pass
over the S[and]B[ank]. Sound[in]gs in 2.1. fath

and 4 feet. Steer right in shore minding the snags.

Snags to be looked out for all the way here.

Rounding the point by a fine large tree and then 2 palms enter a short reach NbyE.

After a point another long reach NbyE. Some small islands open out on the port side. *II N* (*A*). Long reach to a curved point. Great quantity of dangerous snags along the starb[oar]d shore. Follow the slight bend of the shore with caution. The middle of the channel is a S[and]B[ank] always covered.

The more northerly of the 2 islands has its lower end bare of trees covered with grass a[nd] light-green low bushes, then a low flat, and the upper end is timbered with light trees of a darker green tint. A long sandbank unc[overe]d at ½ Full stretches in to the S[ou]th[war]d. No passage inside the islands.

After rounding the point a broad reach opens out towards NNE.

On the port side some small islands. Starboard shore makes a great sweep to the next point.

The middle of this expansion of the river is fouled by extensive sands always covered (Koch).

Follow the bend of the shore keeping pretty well in but not to brush the bank.

Both shores uniform dark-green forest. When nearing the limit point of the reach you will close with some sm[all] islands. Leave them to port. S[and]B[ank] between the islands and the point. Keeping to starboard you get over it in 2.1. fath. Broad bend follows. The direction of the short reach being NNE.

In the bend itself extensive sandbank to be left to port side. Patches on this bank uncovered at ½ F[ull] water.

The channel is pretty wide: there is no necessity in shaving the starboard bank to[o] close. After this a straight long reach on N½E bearing. Keep nearly in the middle but more to starboard. St[arboar]d side islands divided by very

narrow channels on port app[a]r[en]tly one island only. Usual app[earan]ce of dense vegetation dow[n] to water's edge. N[or]th End sm[all]
S[and]B[an]k. 2 fth At the N[or]th end sharp
bend and the broad sweep—NbyE to NEbyN
and N.

To starb[oar]d wide branch dividing islands
before mentionned[10] from m[ai]n land.

IV N

Next reach NNE nearly—Follow the Star-
b[oar]d side now M[ai]n L[an]d river broad—
some app[earan]ce On Starb[oar]d side pass a little narrow branch opening island again. This
reach ends like the last by a straight shore across
its upper end where there is a [word omitted] of
triangular expansion. Next reach nearly North—
after passing the limit point reach nearly north.

A small double island green on the Starb[oar]d
side.

After this first more islands open up with
pretty broad channels between, through which
V.N.   the back shore can be seen—River very broad
here. All the islands are laying [sic] on a line of
bearing about NbyE from the last point. Point
ahead on a bearing ½ a point more northerly.

[A sketch of a reach of the river]

Many large snags along the shores of the islands. Bush and trees to the water's edge. After
passing a narrow island take the channel where
there is a small islet with a conspicuous tree in
the middle of it.

This channel is at first NE then gradually
sweeps up to NbyE and narrows greatly.

After coming out of it you enter a broad expanse with an islet about East and two larger islands with passage between about NNE. [A
sketch representing a reach of the river]

This expanse is bounded to the Eastward by
the M[ai]nland.

Heavy sandb[an]ks show between the further
northern and the upper eastern islands.

The passage is narrow mostly NNE with a
slight easterly bend on its upper end nearly
NEbyN.

The main land is seen right across when coming out to the N[orthw]ard

Passage clear.

VI N.

M[ai]n Land runs nearly N and S. Almost opp[osi]te the Is[lan]d Pass[a]ge there is a wooding place.

Rounding the N[or]th point of the first straight stretch there is a 2[d] elbow and then again a straight N[or]th stretch. To Port there is 3 islands[11] on the bend and another long island further up with some more behind it. On M[ai]n shore after passing a dead stem with a few palms growing near it there is a point with a rocky ledge off it.

The northern expansion of this expansion is perceived with islets and islands. The course is between these and the M[ai]n L[an]d. Off the m[ai]n shore there are rocky ledges under water in several places.

Rocks when the little N[orth]ern islet bears North going along the shore. Many villages on this shore. Leaving all the islands on the Port side cross the mouth of the Loulanga R[iver][12] and steer along m[ai]n shore the reach lying about NbyW½W.

It presents a narrow appearance.

[A sketch of a reach of the river. A dotted line represents the track of the riverboat. One side marked: Shallow S.B., islet; the other side marked: A grassy plain with large trees on the bank; the dotted line marked: *NNW*.]

Loulanga R[iver] and French Factory. Direction *NE*. first reach.

Entering, islet to port. Keep mod[era]te dist[ance] from Star[boar]d shore.

River turns northerly.

To starb[oar]d low circular island. Passage behind. In this back channel is the factory.

Approaching landing mind the stones High bank. Make fast to a tree there. Small, bad land[in]g place. Arr[ived] at F[rench] F[actory] 8[h]15[m] VII N. Left the F[rench] F[actory]

12ʰ45ᵐ (the back island passage through *Lu-langa*).

Leaving the F[ren]ch F[acto]ry steer NNE when clear of round islet facing it and then NNW to enter the narrow channel between two wooded Is[lan]ds, Lulanga left on the starb[oar]d side. Extensive sandbanks to port of you. Pass over in 2 fath or perhaps 9 feet at ½ full water.

The first reach narrow—about NbyW.

Keep in the middle. A short bend NbyE. Nth.VII. The back passage.

[Sketch of a reach with a dotted line representing the boat's track on which following courses are marked: NNW, NWbyN, and N; and soundings in fathoms: 2, and 2. Left shore marked: SB., Grass bank, Bush, and Tresa. Starboard shore marked: grassbank]

The next reach is about NWbyN.

A straight due North—A long bend. Come over to P[or]t Side—snags almost in the middle of passage. A reach due N[or]th.

Another stretch NbyE.

Pass channel to Starb[oar]d leading to Baringu —sand beach facing it stretch towards NbyW Water shallows to 9 and 7 feet.

[Three consecutive pages with sketches forming a rough outline chart of the Lulonga Passage together with sketches on pp. 58 and 61, and then 67 and 69. The dotted line marked: N, N, NbyE, NbyW, NE, NNE, NE, NbyE, and NNE. The bank on the Port Side marked: Grass bk, Bush, Sm beach, Grass, grass. The Starboard Side marked: Snags, To Baringu, Grass swampy, Swamp grass, High bushed point *2ʰ30ᵐ*]

A reach to NE follows. Grassy banks.

Off port bank sand shallows.

After rounding that point channels branch off. Follow the more easterly. Small islet in it.

A long straight about NbyE½E.

Passage broadens out with islands coming in sight.

[A sketch of a part of the Lulonga Passage. The boat's track marked: N½E. On Port Side:

3ʰ30ᵐ. On the Starboard Side: S Bank, S-B, and soundings in fathoms: 2, 2, and 2.]

Steering for a small island bearing N[or]th. Leave it on St[arboar]d Side.

Towards the upper end of it cross over to port avoiding snags Follow the Port shore.

In the elbow must go close in to avoid extensive S[and] B[an]k stretching right in from the island.

Before passing the two small islets get soundings in 2 fath. and less. Keep well inshore. Mind the snags.

A Broad straight NbyE nearly

[The last part of the Lulonga Passage. A dotted line marked: NbyE to NNE. On the Port Side: Snags. Soundings in fathoms: 2, 2, 2, 1, 1, 2, 2, 2, 2. On the Starboard Side: S-Bks.]

When following it must close over to port, avoiding however sunken trees. Passing over tails of the great sandb[an]k with less than one fath[om] up to 2 fath. soundings.

Arriving at the end of this straight cross over on a NE course and enter the main route up the river.

End of Lulanga Pass.

VII.N.

Long NE½N reach; pretty straight. Island to port in a bend of the shore. Off it 2 S[and] B[an]ks on opposite shore with 2 fath at ½ full. Steering along the starb[oar]d bank. Many snags stranded well off the shore.

The point closing this reach on the Port Side has a high tree on it.

After passing this there is a broad straight channel at the end of which no point is seen.

The broad channel runs NbyW.

Sandbanks. Take the narrow channel.

Directly inside camp[in]g place. Indifferent wood.

VIII.N.

A narrow reach about NEbyN.

Left camp at South end of it at 6ʰa.m.

Curve to the NNE and a little broader reach.

The reach expands in a NEbyE direction. To
Port several islands and a small islet bushy on
one end, low on the other. Follow the M[ai]n
Land on the Starb[oar]d side. Great many snags
lining the shore. On the Port Side probably shallow water (K[och]).

At the end of this broad long stretch appear 2
islands.

The little islet to port has a long S[and] B[an]k
on its southern end.

The main shore runs Northeasterly. The next
point to port after pass[in]g the islet has an extensive SE uncovered in places at ½ F[ull]
stretching away along shore to next small island.
From here an island appears in the middle of
river bear[in]g *NNE*.

Steering nearly for it. After passing second
islet to port the river opens out to starboard into
islands laying [sic] NE and SW nearly or a little
more Easterly.

Steer for the middle island about NbyE½E,
then into the broad reach on its port side leaving
it to Starb[oar]d.

Taking this route the M[ai]n Land of the right
bank is left and course taken to left or north
bank. (This is not the usual course, not safe to
follow at less than ½ full water).

IX.N.

Keep a little nearer to the middle island than
to the islands on your Port side. Proceeding cautiously must feel your way in 12 to 8 feet water.
The shore on the port side is the North Bank of
the river.

Snags along but not much off. After passing
two little islands you sight a dead trunk of a tree
and villages begin. In many places cut bank. Excellent wooding places up to the point and in the
great bend. (10ʰ50) *Left 11:30* Rounding the 1st
point after the dead tree you open the 2nd point
bearing ab[ou]t NE where this reach ends. To
Starb[oar]d several islands of which two are
prominent. Land backing there in a semicircle at

IX.N.

a great distance—M[ai]nLand on the S[ou]th Bank not visible.

The river very broad here. Follow close in the bend as there is a large sandbank between the island and the main shore.

Nearing the P[oin]t sounding in 12 to 10 feet (at ½ F.W.)

X.N.

Mind a very bad snag nearly off the point. After a bit of straight shore and a small point ab[ou]t ENE open out 2 small islets come in sight. Steer along the m[ai]n shore. When pass-[in]g the islets much caution and good look out —sandbanks.

[A sketch: the boat's track on a bend of the river and soundings in feet. Also marked: Village, *SB* Cov. ½ F. less 3 feet] Islet N°19.

Following the bend—when approaching the P[oin]t SandB[an]k extends from islet to St[ar-boar]d. A snag stranded on outer edge—pass between the shore and the snag. Another S[and]B[ank] on the point and snags off it. Must steer very close to the bank which is steep to.

River expands broadly here. The general direction of the main shore to the end of the expansion is ENE nearly. For some considerable distance the Starb[oar]d shore is low and grassy. After rounding the shutting in point leave the broad reach and follow the mainland by a narrower channel laying [sic] about NEbyN and turning towards the NE or more easterly still. Coming out of this channel again into the broad part a great number of islands come in sight.

Steer carefully amongst sand bank watching for the edges. Cross over to the island and back to where 2ᵈ village down is. At big clearing cross over again and enter another back passage. Sound[in]gs in 10 to 6 feet. Many snags and some of them right in the fairway.

XII.

Between a long low island and the main sandb[an]ks across with less than 6 feet water over them the passage rather intricate from islet N°19.

The north[er]n end of that pass[a]ge has a
S[and]B[an]k with 10–6 feet of water at ½ F.W.

Coming out of it you follow a broad stretch
on a NEbyE½E course (about) and then keep
off the broad channel to the NE between the
m[ai]nland and an island.

Passage narrow—where it broadens 2 islets in
the bend. One of them has a thin tall dead tree
with one green branch on it. It looks like a
flagstaff with a bough tied up to it at right an-
gles. Steering in always keep closer to the main
shore. Good many nasty snags all along.

After passing the second of the 2 islets you
may notice a third—small. The main shore runs
NEbyE. On the Starb[oar]d side many islands
close together form an almost contin[u]ous
shore.

The channel is not deep from 10 to 6 feet of
water some little distance up after passing the 2d
of two islets.

After that no soundings in *12* feet.

Several small islets on the Starb[oar]d side.

On the islands on the Starb[oar]d side good
many dead palms.

Further on a sandbank right across: *6–10 feet*.

At large clearing stopped. Firewood. Snags.

XIII. Left at 6h30m A straight reach NE½N.
When approaching the P[oin]t (to Port) ending
the straight steer over to the other side to avoid
sandbank.

On starb[oar]d side small islets in the bights of
the shore, which is composed of long islands
overlapping each other and appearing like one
land when steaming up the river.

XIII.N.

Round in back again in 9 feet of water.

Following the main shore care should be taken
to avoid snags which are stranded right along it
in great quantities. *2d reach* before coming to
end of it cross over to the island 20. Right close
in to the upp[e]r end—in 9 to 5 feet. Sandbank
off the main shore. Pass close point on star-
b[oar]d side and steer to leave next island on
starb[oar]d side *nearly* in midchannel. Sandbank

on the m[ai]n shore—Cross over to upper end of vill[a]ge clearing. Follow the shore—Opposite sm[a]ll beach in isl[an]d to starb[oard] sound-[in]gs 9 feet. After passing this, steer off the m[ai]n shore and steer across in 9 to 5 feet to leave the sm[a]ll islet to port. Keep nearly in the middle when entering the pass[a]ge, then steer rather over to starb[oar]d shore (big island). *Snags.* Coming out of the back channel you sight a very [word missed] clearing bearing N[or]th. Steer a little below it passing over 10 feet sound[in]gs. When nearing the bank water deepens.

Follow the cut bank pretty close. Safe. No snags there—Half round reach following in a EbyN direction. Forest. Snags again. Keep a little out. A long small islet hardly noticeable before coming to the closing P[oin]t on P[or]t side. *Sound[in]gs 10 feet.*

Another bend where you keep nearly in the middle. *10 feet S[oun]d[in]gs* in one place.

This bend terminates in a NE direction.

There is now a double channel—one broad about EbyN, another narrow nearly NE. Leave the island to starb[oard] and follow its inner shore to take the narrow p[assa]ge. Sound[in]gs 9 to 5 feet.

This passage is between the m[ai]n land on Port side and 2 islands on starb[oar]d. Where the 1st is[lan]d finishes there is a sandbank. Steering close in to the islands in s[ou]nd[ing]s 10 to 5 feet—Steer over to M[ai]n shore and back again. All the way about 7 feet of water. Less in places.

After leaving this narrow passage and rounding the point another similar passage presents itself—Keep nearly in the middle where *7 to 9 feet water* are obtained at ½ F[ull] W[ater].

Another narrow passage presenting the same features, only a little narrower. About 10 feet of water—Passage ends on an Eastern bearing.

Coming out of this last the main stream is entered. River broadens. This is the upper end of the northern bank passage.[13]

XV.

Notes to the Up-river Book

1. Ludwig Rasmus Koch (1865–1906), a Dane, captain of the *Roi des Belges* (N. Sherry, p. 400).
2. Soundings, in fathoms.
3. This sentence lightly crossed out. Lawson River is named Mbali on newer maps.
4. Time not entered.
5. Bolobo, a mission established in 1886 by the well-known missionary George Grenfell.
6. At Irebu, opposite the mouth of the Ubangi.
7. Not entered.
8. At Bolenge.
9. Usually: Ruki, or Rouki, River.
10. After the French *mentionné*.
11. From the French *Il y a trois isles*.
12. Correctly: Lulonga.
13. *Roi des Belges* crossed the Equator in the morning of August 16. She arrived the same day at the mouth of the Lulonga, leaving on August 17 early afternoon. Then there are two overnight stops mentioned, and by the evening of August 19 the boat must have reached Bangala (or Nouvelle-Anvers, N 1′36″ E 19′07″)—as indicated in the title of the second part of the Up-river Book.

To begin a novel or short story and then lay it aside for some time—for months or even years—was quite common in Conrad's thorny writing career: it happened so with *The Rescue, Lord Jim, Chance, Suspense* and others. But only in one instance did he put away a work and never take it up again: this was the case of *The Sisters*.

It was to be his third novel and he began it after finishing *An Outcast of the Islands,* in autumn or early winter 1895. It is a pity that in Conrad's preserved letters to his good friend and distant cousin Mme. Marguerite Poradowska, there is a five-year gap, beginning in June 1895, because the origins of the story are somehow connected with her. Poradowska made her debut eight years before Conrad and published several novels with Polish and Ukrainian backgrounds. In February 1895, Conrad wrote to her that he admired her descriptions of the Ukrainian fields; Conrad also describes those fields in *The Sisters*. On June 11, in the last extant letter to her of that year, he wrote longingly about Poradowska being "among the birds" in her house in Passy, a Paris suburb.[1] The action of *The Sisters* culminates in the same suburb, and our last glimpse of the hero juxtaposes him with a colony of blackbirds.

The preserved fragment of *The Sisters* consists of seven short chapters and tells two separate stories. The first four sections concern a young painter from Russia (but not a Russian: he is at least half Ukrainian). He wanders around Western Europe, restless and increasingly disillusioned; finally he decides to settle in Passy. The remaining three sections introduce two sisters, orphans of Basque origin. The younger of them is being brought up by her uncle—also in Passy. The tale is interrupted before the protagonists meet or even become aware of each other's existence. In the second part similarities are easily noticeable with *The Arrow of*

Gold, a supposedly autobiographical novel which Conrad wrote over twenty years later. Both works present two sisters born in the Pyrenees, with the same names, Rita and Teresa, and also with a fanatical Basque priest for an uncle. In both stories their families are staunchly royalist-Carlist. However, in *The Arrow of Gold* Doña Rita, the hero's love, is a former paramour of a rich French painter, Henry Allégre, and her character seems entirely different.

Ford Madox Ford, who wrote an introduction to the first edition of *The Sisters* in 1928, has some ideas about the intended subject of the novel (incestuous love) and the reasons why Conrad put it aside (difficulty in handling the character of the priest). But there is no reason to believe that Conrad even talked to Ford (who usually found the truth too tedious to stick to) about *The Sisters*. He worked on this piece three and half years before meeting Ford for the first time. It is also evident that Ford did not read the text very attentively; he did not even notice the parallels with *The Arrow*. It is hardly possible and rather useless to take most of his pronouncements seriously. However, he is right in suggesting a likeness between some passages in *The Sisters* and the short story "The Return," which Conrad wrote a couple of years later. In both we see attempts at introspection, and in both encounter similarly vapid psychological expatiation. Ford confesses that he "has always liked" "The Return," but he is almost completely alone in this sentiment. Conrad himself felt very uneasy about the story, surely one of his weaker pieces.

It is clear enough that *The Sisters* belongs to Conrad's apprenticeship. Divergent and unintegrated inspirations are openly at work. There are numerous Byronic associations (although Stephen is too inert to be a Byronic hero): Stephen leaves his homeland, wanders disconsolately around Europe—weary with life but independent in spirit, without friends, becomes rich, and is exploited by spongers, compares Art and Nature, etc.; there is even one direct allusion to *Childe Harold's Pilgrimage*. Echoes of Maupassant and Daudet are not difficult to hear. Polish literary tradition also makes itself strongly felt. This last element is, of course, the most elusive for an English-speaking reader, but it gives the story its most memorable fragments: descriptions of landscape and scenes from the life of Stephen's parents. Both sound as if faithfully transplanted, the former from Polish romantic poetry, the latter from realistic fiction of the middle of the century—or simply from the Memoirs of Conrad's uncle and guardian, Tadeusz Bobrowski.[2] And both concern things Conrad knew and remembered well: he had been *there* just three years before! By contrast, almost everything else in the story sounds contrived, and almost everything else is surely a product of the imagination.

English and American critics have been impressively unanimous in their low estimation of *The Sisters*. Beginning with Garnett, who advised Conrad to drop the story, nobody has had a good word for it. The main target of scorn has been, and quite justly, the style. Particularly the style of the psychological and abstract passages, which are uniformly elusive and at the same time pompously strained. The text abounds in misty generalities ("I want to know . . . don't ask what— what some others knew and died without telling. Till I know I cannot come back.") and lame metaphors ("They [deserts] also would speak in glorious promises only to cast him down at last from the pinnacle of his expectations"). Descriptions, too, sometimes sound incongruous, as in the passage where Parisian grass is represented in terms of all-devouring tropical flora.

In Poland, however, *The Sisters* was greatly prized. To a large extent this was due to translation, not only because it was a very good one, but primarily because *The Sisters* simply reads better in Polish than in English. The syntax, loose and contrived, becomes natural and even limpid in a word-by-word rendering.

As hardly any English and American critic knows Polish, Conrad's stylistic oddities are usually credited to the influence of French. However, a closer examination almost always reveals that a strange-sounding sentence can be translated into correct Polish without so much as one change in the order and mutual relation of words. There are many—too many— sentences like that in *The Sisters*.

The influence on Conrad of the imagery, descriptive techniques, and moral and political themes characteristic of Polish romantic poetry has been commented upon several times although it is rarely remembered by critics.[3] It is clearly noticeable in *The Sisters:* we can almost feel the pressure of Polish literary tradition on Conrad's consciousness and language. And it is, to a degree, a harmful pressure: Conrad's style sounds artificial and he is obviously unable to come to grips with his protagonist. Perhaps we should rather reverse the

order and say that the main snag in the story is the hero himself, presented in such a fumbling way that it is impossible to
take him seriously, or even to visualize what he might have
been were he more vividly described.

There are several hypotheses explaining Conrad's decision
to drop *The Sisters*. None of them sounds fully satisfactory.
Jocelyn Baines supposes that Conrad acted on Edward Garnett's advice, justified because the story "reads like a pains-
taking exercise in the art of fine writing."[4] True enough, but
why was the text so bad? Why was Conrad writing worse
than before and after? Albert J. Guérard believes that *The
Sisters* contains "woolly rhetoric and oblique embarrassed
self-justifications of autobiography imperfectly transposed,"
and that the material and the method did not suit Conrad.[5]
Quite right, probably; but again: why didn't they suit him?
After all, he was writing about subjects freely chosen and not
too distant. Thomas Moser sees in *The Sisters* one more
proof that love was Conrad's "uncongenial subject": "Conrad
seems to have tried to write a sympathetic account of love between two whites; he discovered quickly (in less than six
months) that he could not."[6] However, it is just a supposition
that there was to be in *The Sisters* a love affair sympa-
thetically told; and there is nothing about love in the first
seven chapters, which are unquestionably poor. Stephen is
not an unconvincing character because he is an unconvincing
lover.

We should, I believe, start by asking another question:
Why did Conrad *begin* to write *The Sisters*—i.e., why did he
decide to write such a novel?

Almayer's Folly and *An Outcast of the Islands* were quite
well received by reviewers, but rather coolly by readers.
Conrad wanted to strike at something more popular; but at
the same time he was afraid of becoming an "exotic" writer:
he set himself more serious aims and rigorous standards.
Looking around for subjects familiar, intriguing, and at the
same time non-English—the hapless "Return" excluded, he
felt sufficiently certain of himself to take up an English theme
only ten years later, with *The Secret Agent*—he evidently
resolved to make use of his knowledge of France and the
Carlists on the one hand, and of Eastern Europe on the
other.

The Eastern part of the scheme proved his undoing. He
could not decide to write about Poland: that, apparently, was

too painful, or too close, or in some other way too difficult—
or perhaps he thought, probably justly, that nobody would be
interested.[7] Therefore, with a sudden display of naïveté,[8] he
chose to adopt a hero from southern Russia. For some ambi-
tious reason, he wished his character to be an artist. To make
him a writer would have been risky, would have strongly
suggested autobiography; therefore, he commanded Stephen
to be a painter. That was another false step, as Conrad knew
very little about the visual arts. Consequently, Stephen's
thoughts about his vocation are abstruse and desperately
hazy.

Locating the action on the Continent turned out to be right
only in theory. Conrad's continental experiences were definitely not experiences of an Englishman. It was certainly
easier for him to write in English about places from which
he brought back memories couched in that language.[9]

Still, the main reason of the failure, the main obstacle in
developing the story, was Stephen with his national and
cultural background. Paul Kirschner, who mistakenly takes
Stephen for a Russian, believes that Conrad is "writing from
the inside," that he identifies with the hero, and that "the
view of the West under Eastern eyes is not flattering."[10] Certainly, flattering it is not, but the criticism is expressed in
vague and banal terms. The point is that Conrad could share
with his character only the reminiscences of their mutual, but
nationally and culturally divided, homeland. He could not
know his ideas, family relations, feelings, interests; he had
little knowledge of the life of Ukrainians and Russians, of
their moral and political sentiments, of their religious and
artistic traditions. His background as a Pole, a member of
land-owning nobility, a Catholic, from a family of freedom
fighters, was completely different. To make up for his ignorance by an effort of imagination turned out to be impossible;
he was not writing a naïvely picturesque, exotic story as
Poradowska would, and he knew the subject less well than
she did.

The motif of disillusionment with the West is common in
Polish nineteenth-century literature. But it is disenchantment
of a specific kind, expressed in concrete political and social
terms, usually in the form of accusations that Western
Europe is politically opportunist and crudely materialistic,
that it forgets, for the sake of economic gain, the great causes

of freedom and equality. Attacks on indifference to the plight of suppressed nations, standard in the writings of several Poles Conrad knew personally, were to him of no avail in his novel. And what an obscure Ukrainian could feel when faced with Western art and culture, Conrad was simply unable to visualize.

With every paragraph he must have faced anew the same dilemma; whether to make the hero more real by endowing him with his own consciousness and knowledge, and by so doing change him and the book completely—or to stick to the original conception and plod ahead through clumsy banalities. There was no good way out. The sisters he could, perhaps, somehow manipulate; but Stephen—especially when he ended his elusive wanderings, settled down in Passy and had to be tackled at a close distance—was not to be managed. This book simply would not let itself be written.

An artistic failure, *The Sisters* remains a fascinating piece. The fragment presents dramatic evidence of Conrad's search for his own place in life and his own line in literature.

*

The whereabouts of the manuscript of *The Sisters* is presently unknown. The text published here is based on the 1928 edition (Crosby Gaige, New York, 935 copies), which has a preface by Ford Madox Ford.

Notes

1. Conrad to Poradowska, ed. Gee and Sturm, pp. 91 and 98.
2. These memoirs were published only in 1900 (Tadeusz Bobrowski, *Pamiętniki*, vols. I–II, Lwów), but Conrad probably knew their content much earlier.
3. The most important of these poets are: Adam Mickiewicz (1798–1855), Juliusz Słowacki (1809–49) and Zygmunt Krasiński (1812–59). Cf. Zdzisław Najder, Introduction to *Conrad's Polish Background*, 1964; Andrzej Busza, *Conrad's Polish Literary Background*, Roma–London, 1966; Adam Gillon, "Some Polish Literary Motifs in the Works of Joseph Conrad," *Slavic and East European Journal*, X (Winter 1966), pp. 424–39.
4. Jocelyn Baines, pp. 167–68.
5. Albert J. Guérard, *Conrad the Novelist*, Harvard University Press, 1958, p. 93.
6. Thomas Moser, *Joseph Conrad: Achievement and Decline*, Harvard University Press, 1957, p. 62.

7. Edward Garnett, Introduction to *Letters from Joseph Conrad,* Indianapolis, 1928, p. 6. Jessie Conrad, *Joseph Conrad and His Circle,* New York, 1935, pp. 49–50.

8. Similarly, he gave his first son a typically Russian name, Borys—acting under an illusion that it is a name used in the Ukraine and by Poles living there as well.

9. As late as January 1907 he wrote to Poradowska: "And English is, too, still a foreign language to me, requiring an immense effort to handle." Gee and Sturm, p. 109.

10. Paul Kirschner, *Conrad: the Psychologist as Artist,* Edinburgh, 1968, p. 262. Stephen's mother came from a village on the Dnieper, and his father called him a Cossack, which also suggests Ukrainian origin.

The Sisters

I

For many years Stephen had wandered amongst the cities of Western Europe. If he came from the East—if he possessed the inborn wisdom of the East—yet it must be said he was only a lonely and inarticulate mage, without a star and without companions. He set off on his search for a creed—and found only an infinity of formulas. No angel's voice spoke from above to him. Instead, he heard, right and left, the vociferations of idle fanatics extolling this path or that with earthly and hoarse voices that rang out, untrustworthy, in empty darkness. And he heard also the soft murmur of lazy babblers whispering deferential promises of greatness in exchange for the generous hospitality of that Russian painter who had roubles. From Berlin to Dresden, from Dresden to Vienna, to many other places, then to cities of Italy, at last back to Munich he travelled on, trying to read a meaning into all the forms of beauty that solicited his admiration. He thought he understood the language of perfection. Did it not uplift his thoughts like the wind of heaven that sends sunward in a soaring cloud the dust of the arid earth? But like the wind the meaning seemed to be elusive and formless. The sweetness of the voice intoxicated him with pure delight, but the message sounded as if delivered in declaration of incomprehensible things, with a reserve of final clearness, with an incompleteness of emotion that made him doubt the heavenly origin of that voice. The prodigies of chisel and brush transported him at first with the hope of a persuasion, of an unveiled religion of art—and then plunged him into despair by refusing to say the last word. He turned to men—to all kinds of men—and it seemed to him that similar to the angels and the devils of mediaeval cathedrals, they were all carved of the same stone, that they were enigmatical, hard and without heart. Neither the dead nor the living would speak intelligibly to him. At times he mourned over his own want of intelligence. He believed that in the world of art, amongst so many forms of created beauty, there could be found the secret of genius. All those brains that had produced so many masterpieces had left amongst them, hidden from the crowd, but visible to the elect, the expression of their creed: the one, the final, the appeasing. He looked for it; he looked for the magic sign in all the galleries—in all the cathedrals from Rome to Cologne. In many towns he lingered, sometimes alone, sometimes in the midst of other seekers whom he loved for the sake of their quest and whom he despised a little, because it seemed to him dishonest to accept—as they did—the disconnected mutterings of common men as the voice of inspired prophets. He despised those believers only a little, and that not always. He had doubts. Instead of deceiving themselves to make life easy, had they not perchance obtained that message which, year after year, eluded his longing? Who knows! He began to doubt his own aspirations. They presented themselves sometimes to him as a plot of the powers of darkness for the destruction of his soul. Then he would rush out of himself into the world. The Western life captivated him by the amplitude of its complicated surface, horrified him by the interior jumble of its variegated littleness. It was full of endeavour, of feverish effort, of endless theories, of preconceived hates, of misplaced loves. It was all limited, hard, sharp in outline, unlovely in form. And so were the men. They boasted of the crystalline purity of their horizon. He saw that it was pure as crystal and as impenetrable; that under its dome there was nothing great because all was very finite, definite, bound to the earth, imprisoned within those so pellucid and so infamous walls on the other side of which there was the august world of the infinite, the Eternal; that other world always invoked by these men yet never desired, falsely extolled, worshipped, invoked by the lips—and always hopelessly remote from those unquiet hearts in which its mystery could awake nothing but secret fear, or more secret scorn.

But mostly he sought refuge from the reproach of his impotence in ardent work. This, consolatory in its assertion of what he could do, had its periods of discouragement too—by placing face to face with his limitations that man who strove after the illimitable. He would look to no one as teacher. He stood aloof from the world. But he took his stand in it. He had need of it. He had need to see the hollow enthusiasms and to hear the ring of empty words round him, if for nothing else but to steady this wavering trust in his own convictions. Associating with many, he communed with none. He was generally taciturn. People asked: "Who's that fellow? He does nothing. He does not even talk." Rarely they heard him, and then answered their own question by the easy solution of an epithet: "madman" or "humbug." The few who had seen his work assured the others that he was perfectly "impossible." Some said: "He is too rich to ever be anything." A few murmured the damning word of "Dreamer." Nobody quite said: "Fool." Almost all lived with him on terms of current friendship. The fellow had money and would never be dangerous; he had no talent. A verdict deadly and final, like the knife of a guillotine. Only a small band of the good and the smart hated him. It is hard to say why, exactly. Either because he would not talk to them the jargon of the craft, or, more probably, a correct instinct of his value had been vouchsafed to them as a reward of so much smartness and so much virtue. Doubtless they would not have been so bitter and would have condescended at last to break his sumptuous bread had they known then how short his life, how faint his trace on the earth, was fated to be.

Far away, beyond many great rivers in wood-built and dusty cities of the steppe, Stephen's father and mother waited for his letters. These came regularly four times a year. And for many days the father would carry the last missive in his bosom, somewhere inside his shirt, like a scapulary, because it was from his eldest son, from that son who had been destined in his thoughts to attain the rank of a general. The mother would weep silently with no other trouble but that of his absence. They were two peasants. She was the daughter of a village elder, from the banks of the Dnieper.

He was a liberated man born in the neighborhood who had wandered away, shrewd and restless, from his hamlet and became afterwards, from very small beginnings, a merchant of the first guild —a very rich man. But however rich, he always remained a peasant, a man with a beard. He was cunning, naïve, unscrupulous, believing and tender-hearted. He gave largely in charity and would sometimes stand on the steps of the church chatting with a beggar and calling him "Brother" without the slightest affectation, as a matter of course. All men are brothers. When reproving his two pale and scrofulous clerks (that was the extent of his establishment; he did almost everything himself) he prefaced his remarks by the exclamation: "Thou! son of a dog," without the faintest spark of animosity in his heart. He feared God, venerated the saints, bowed at every opportunity to holy images, crossed himself rapidly, with three bunched fingers, an incalculable number of times, on fitting occasions—and would perjure his soul for three roubles with an innocent smile, like a little child fibbing before an indulgent father. He obtained government contracts. He amassed money. He became known in the government offices—even in the capital—where he could be seen standing at the doors, cap in hand, with a propitiatory face. Bull-necked officials in tight green uniforms addressed him—from armchairs—with caressing condescension as: "Thou little thief! O! thou perfect liar." He was not spoiled by the commendations of the great. He gave bribes. He was greatly esteemed. He became necessary to many. He remained unassuming—the peasant of old days.

Theirs had been a love match. She was the beauty of the village, daughter of a rich man; he was looked upon as a wandering ne'er-do-well of colossal presumption. They fell in love violently with each other. They ran away. They never regretted it. In the early days (when the passions are strong) he beat her a little once or twice, just to place firmly the fact of his affection beyond the possibility of even the most fleeting doubt. Ever after, he treated her in a grave, contained manner, with a patriarchal superiority of indulgence. She thought of him as the greatest of men and of herself as the happiest of women. They passed through some hard times. The father-in-law, almost unforgiving, would do nothing for the vagabond beyond giving him an old wooded cart and a pair of shaggy and diminutive horses. In that equipage they hawked from town to town the watermelons of central Russia. The first child—the son Stephen—was born in the casual shelter of a roadside hut; and before he was a fortnight old they were again on the road. The woman sat on some rotten mats, perched high in the sunlight on top of the pile of fruit. The man trudged with silent footsteps in bark shoes, by the drooping heads of his horses, and glanced over his shoulder at the mother from time to time. Sometimes the great weariness of the limitless expanse of the plain would penetrate his very soul. Then he would turn half round—not stopping —and shout cheerily: "How is our Kossak,[1] Malanya; our brave boy?" And she would answer, from above the cloud of dust, in a high-pitched—not yet a very strong—voice: "He is getting on beautifully, Sydor!"

At night they often camped outside a village. With the mats and the cart, Sydor would make a shelter for his wife. If the night was fine they sat through the evening in the open. Long before its lips could shape a word, the baby's eyes had been turned, untrammeled, towards the great heaven. The father and the mother, sitting by a small fire, conversed in murmurs. On a thin sheet of coarse linen, spread over the scanty grass of the roadside, lay the child—open-eyed and quiet. Peasants' children seldom cry. They seem to be born with a prescience of the inutility of lament. With a child's fearless stare Stephen's eyes exchanged placid and profound glances with the inscrutable stars. Ignorant and undismayed, he stretched his unsteady little hands towards the universe in a desire to play with that brilliant dust which streams through infinite space into an infinity of time. The glory of heaven is very near a child's soul, as the memory of his land is near the heart of an exile at the beginning of his pilgrimage. Afterwards the withering wisdom of the earth destroys the dreamy memories and longings in the awakening of a peal of laughter or a sigh of pain.

Stephen, unwinking, looked on—smiled at Immensity. In the daytime, from his mother's arms, he scrutinized with inarticulate comprehension the vast expanse of the limitless and fertile blacklands nursing life in their undulating bosom under the warm caress of sunshine. In the shallow folds of the plain dammed streams

overflowed into an unruffled glimmer of small lakes, placid, as
though soothed by the whispering tenderness of encircling reeds.
On their banks dark willows and slim, unsteady birches stirred in
the gentle and powerful breath of the indolent steppe. Here and
there a clump of low oaks looked sombre and stolid, planted
firmly above the dark patch of its own shade. On the slope hung a
village, scattered white huts, with high, ragged, thatched roofs
under which small unequal windows twinkled, like small eyes of a
band of deformed and humorous dwarfs winking under high caps
cavalierly aslant. Amongst them the green cupola of a village
church, held up on high against the sky the gleam of a gilt cross.
The cart would run down the declivity, dash through a troop of
dogs barking about the wheels, rumble with loose traces over the
dam—and go on slowly, with patient straining of the shaggy
horses to climb the rise on the other side. As it laboriously topped
the ridge the wide plains would open out again with the overpowering suddenness of a revelation. The uniform level of ripe wheat
stretched out into unbounded distances, immensely great, filled by
the hum of invisible life of the infinitely little: one unbroken mur-
muring field, as big as a world, spread out under the unclouded silence of the sky. Far off on the line of horizon, another village
showed above the monotony of yellow corn, the green path of its
few trees, and lay lone, minute and brilliant, like an emerald
negligently dropped on the sands of a limitless and deserted shore.

II

The fabulous vastness of the country repeated itself day after day
with the persistence of eternal truth—sank into the child's uncon-
sciousness, coloured his childish thoughts, his young feelings,
carried persuasion into his ignorance—irresistible like an unceas-
ing whisper of a voice from Heaven. The father's prosperity grew
apace—quicker than the child. There are such fortunate hazards!
They ceased to wander and the boy lived with his Ukrainian
mother in riverside towns while the father travelled about, busy
with his wheat transport contracts, watching, high-booted in the
mire of banks, his blunt-nosed scows afloat on the muddy streams
of interminable waterways. In the desolation of the antechambers
of government offices he found a new ambition for his son. He
saw him uniformed, embroidered, bemedalled, autocratic, called

Excellency. Everything is possible in Russia; and, as the proverb says: anything may be done—only cautiously![2] When the boy was eight years old he put him to school in a provincial town. From there Stephen went to the capital. The elder man could not understand the ambition of the youth . . . Paint! Why paint? Paint what? Where? What's the good of it? Generals don't paint; nor do Councillors—even the writers in chancelleries don't paint. As to the General-Governors they would not even speak to a painter; they would not hear him if he presumed to. . . . The old man was afraid of such an incomprehensible form of madness. The son took his stand on the autocracy of vocation and argued his point in strange words, with bewildering arguments. The father saw only the fixedness of resolve and—in his fear of losing the favourite for ever—pleaded timidly. . . . All the painters of which his son spoke—he understood—were dead. Well! Poor folk, God rest their souls. What's the good, then, of going abroad if there was no one there to tell the secrets of the trade. They had left works? Maybe, maybe. He felt certain Stephen could paint much better than those dead fellows. Then, why go so far to look at what they left—if there was anything left to look at? He doubted it. Such a long time—long time. Things get rotten and crumble—houses and bridges—let alone paintings. And they were foreigners too! Why go so far—amongst Germans and such like? Was Russia not big enough to paint in—if he must! . . . He bowed his head at last. Heaven willed it. For his sins! For his sins! . . . "And do you write to us—we are old people," he said to his son. Then added with a tremulous sense of his own cunning, "Write to us. You will be here and there—God knows! Write so that we know where to send money after you. Those foreigners are great cheats and you are young—young. Well, it's time. Then, go with God . . . and come back soon." They embraced. The son drove off, the big collar of his cloak up, without turning his head once. In the house the mother had thrown her print skirt over her head and wept in the profound darkness of her grief. The father stood at the gate and threw a rapid sign of the cross after the vanished longings of his simple heart.

For years, under the gilded domes of splendid cathedrals, in the imposing gloom of holy monasteries, or in humble village churches the bereaved father sought in vain the help of renowned

saints who answered his trustful prayers by the meaningless stare
of naïve art. Evidently he did not deserve the mercy of the
blessed. This thought dawned upon him at last, and he ceased to
make himself obtrusive by his prayers but still haunted as-
siduously the sacred edifices in an indistinct but tenacious hope
that the sight of his mute distress would, in time, move some at-
tendant at the footstool of the Most High to a compassionate in-
tercession. With both elbows on the little wooden table of "Trak-
tirs"[3] frequented by men of his class he often told his friends,
while they sipped their tea, the story of his great sorrow—ending
it solemnly with the words: "Our son is under the visitation of
God," and with a deep sigh. He cursed the impious Frenchmen
who had, by their black arts, bewitched the boy. After consulting
his wife he made a solemn vow to build a church in which the
misguided son could have his peace with God by painting, on a
golden background, a gorgeous altarpiece. Let him only return!
The money was ready! But Providence, unlike the powers of this
earth, was impervious to the offer of a splendid bribe. He did not
see his son again. Reaching home, after one of his business journeys, he was seized by some violent internal disorder. He had just
time in the last return of consciousness to assure his distracted
wife of his belief that the Jews had poisoned all the wells in the
province—and expired in her arms with the resignation of indifference. She followed him quickly. During the last months of her
life she seemed to have forgotten her eldest boy in an impatient
longing to rejoin the man who had charmed her youth.

Stephen grieved, and carried his grief, contained and profound,
through every second of the first few weeks. In the sifted light
coming with pearly purity through the white clouds of lofty
skylights he wandered with slow steps in the long galleries between the masterpieces of line and colour. The atmosphere of
these places was full of the heartless serenity of perfection. The
other people in them looked to him very small, distinct and—no
matter how numerous—exceedingly lonely, like men and women
lost in a strange world. Their irresolute footsteps rang, sharp but
ineffectual, in the significant silence of glorious memories. Stephen
wandered about. His powerful and clumsy frame clad in black at-
tracted attention, eluded it by its restlessness. He flitted in the
doorways, crossed the narrow end of long perspectives, was seen,

thrown in abandoned postures, on circular couches, only to get up again and pace forward stiffly with fixed and unseeing eyes. The whispers of amused remarks did not disturb him—were not heard by him. The first appeal of death vivifies the past, evokes a great clearness of distinct memories out of the crash of destroyed hopes. Stephen remembered, could see, the pathetic faces of the dead who—he imagined—had died with his name on their lips. The armour of his art, the armour polished, impenetrable, unstained and harder than steel, seemed to be stripped off him by a mighty hand, to fall with an ominous clatter at his feet. Defenceless, he was pierced by the venomous sharpness of remorse. He had abandoned those two loving hearts for the promise of unattainable things, for alluring lies, for beautiful illusions. He wanted to shout at immortal achievements: "You have no heart." To his lofty aspirations he said: "You have no conscience." To Beauty: "Thou art a lie!" To Inspiration: "Go! Depart with the last word unspoken—for I have no more sacrifices to offer." In the haste of his regrets he dispersed with frenzied renunciation the band of charming phantoms that had for so many years surrounded his life—and remained alone, humbled and appalled by the reality of his loss.

This state of agonizing self-reproach did not last long—no longer than with other men. Stephen's brother wrote him letters where filial sorrow was mingled with judicious concern about their affairs. That young man was cheery, practical and brotherly. He had taken over the business. He was also modern and irreverent. He spoke with strange levity of the Governor of the Province saying that the fellow had priest's eyes—that see everything—and a wolf's maw—that would swallow everything.[4] "But"—he added—"I have the wherewithal to stuff his maw and have obtained the lease of government mills. We shall make a good thing of it. And next year I go to the Caucasus—provisioning the troops—where we shall dwell in a town, Brother, in a big town! You come and live with us. You shall paint those Tcherkesses and the Georgian women, and make money by it—if you like. There's a fellow here—went to Turkestan; painted those savages there on small bits of canvas, and even paper—and everybody in Petersburg is running to see. It's true! I have seen myself people fight at the doors. There's many mad folks in our country. Why shouldn't you get

some of their roubles? But there is plenty of money already. Half
of it is yours. I understand affairs. Come and live with us. My wife
asks after you often and your nephew is beginning to run about.
There's no country in the world like our country. Come!"

III

Stephen, letter in hand, looked across space and time at the
land of his birth. From afar it looked immense, mysterious—and
mute. He was afraid of it. He was afraid of the silent dawn of life,
he who sought amongst the most perfect expressions of matured
thought the word that would fling open the doors of beyond. Not
there! Not there! . . . He wrote to his brother: "I cannot return.
You would not understand if I tried to explain. But, believe me, to
return now they are dead would be worse than suicide, which is
the unpardonable crime. I want to know . . . don't ask what—
what some others knew and died without telling. Till I know I
cannot come back. I think I dare to hope that when the word is
spoken, I shall understand. Do not wonder at what I say. It is useless. You are right. There is no country like our country and no
people like us—peasants. We are God's children. Little children
yet. If we were like the men are around me now I could not speak
to you as I am speaking. We are Brothers. We are different, but
we love without understanding one another—and we trust. Do not
be angry. If there is money, tell me how much there is for me for I
must arrange my life. I could also earn it—but then I would have
to give up my hope. Many men had to do it. It wouldn't matter—
but still I am anxious to know. Cherish our land—preserve in
your heart the simplicity God's mercy has put there—think of me
often."

The brother returned a puzzled but a resigned answer. Into
business matters he went thoroughly with great clearness and
Stephen found himself almost rich or, at any rate, in very comfortable circumstances. He had recovered somewhat from the terrible
shock of his loss. The black violence of grief faded after a time
into a cold greyness: the pale and unwilling dawn of another short
day of uncertain respites. In that ashy light in which at that time
he lived Stephen saw his phantom companions return, beckon,
smile, point onwards with shadowy arms; and he heard the ghostly

whisper of alluring words shaped by their beautiful and unreal lips. He must go! He had paid an enormous price for the privilege of a hopeless strife! Was it hopeless? . . . As he lay on a couch, with half-closed eyes, in the silence of his studio, the shadows of the evening closed round him. The day was attuning itself slowly to the sorrowful note of his heart. He got up, walked irresolutely about. The big room was under the roof which, over a part of it, came low down, with glazed openings that resembled slanting and luminous trapdoors. He walked there bending low and put his head out of the window by the simple process of standing up again. He saw the blurred waste of jumbled roofs and, further on, the rectilinear contours of a distant building shamming under a clouded sky the dignity of some Greek temple. Just beyond, the rounded masses of clumps of trees in the park with here and there a poplar shooting up like a spire, seemed to protest emotionally, with an indignant tremble of all their curves, against the rigid purity of that lie. Round his head, innumerable sparrows twittered aggressively, hopping amongst chimney-stacks. The world appeared ugly, colourless and filled with the impertinent, personal chatter of small impudences. He drew back abruptly as if to avoid a damaging contact. For a long time he meditated, sometimes striding slowly, at times standing motionless amongst canvases where the advancing night had erased the vestiges of his persevering attempts to disclose his soul to himself and to others. He thought: It is dark now but tomorrow is another day. I have found no living teacher—and the dead will not speak. Why? . . . I have offered to them the awful sacrifice of two human hearts. Is it not enough? Am I unworthy? Who knows? And yet, and yet I feel . . . "Very well," he muttered with a wave of his hand towards the sham temple where immortal masterpieces kept their secret, unmoved before the insincere ecstasies of the blind. "Very well. Be mute. Yours would have been, after all, but a human voice. I will go to the source from which you spring—to the origin of all Inspiration . . ." After a while he murmured indistinctly, "Nature," as if he had been ashamed of using the profaned word —the word bedraggled on so many lips—to clothe the august form of the terrible, of the immense and tormenting Idea.

He left suddenly, without seeing anybody, without making even an attempt to shake the ever-ready hands of casual companions;

whereby he caused his departure to be much discussed and the
qualification of "a beastly plutocrat" added to every mention of
his name, for about a week or so—in fact till he became utterly
forgotten. He was not a man to leave a mark on the minds of his
contemporaries; for he, strange monster, had not been provided
with that touch of commonplace which makes us all brothers—
and some of us illustrious. His work lay yet in the future, his lips
were mute—and he pushed his aimless way through youthful
crowds leaving no trail: unless a faint sense of hostility, awakened
in some well-ordered minds, may be put down to his account for a
memorable distinction.

Again he travelled south. But this time he left the towns aside
and looked at the uncovered face of the world. From the windows
of commodious hotels he looked at the mountains and loathed
them. They repelled him. They seemed to him senseless and
wicked, like magnificent monuments erected to the frenzied vio-
lences of some dark and terrible past. In the valleys he could not
breathe, and the sunrises seen from lofty summits he had climbed
in his search disclosed to his sight only a disorderly mob of peaks
whose shapes were as fantastic and aimless as a fevered dream.
The Creator had tossed and jumbled that tormented bit of universe with an angry hand into a hopeless wilderness: forbidding
and dumb.

Stephen left the mountains and sought Nature in other aspects.
And he saw her washed, brushed, fenced in, tricked out;
artificially harmonious or artificially dishevelled, such as a super-
civilized actress personating a gypsy, with the scent of manufac-
tured perfumes lingering under the dainty and picturesque rags.
Even in the most remote and wildest places where he set up his
easel, the hand of man seemed to raise an unscalable wall between
him and his Maker. He was discouraged. At last he turned his
face to the west, towards the sea.

There, the opening of a wide horizon touched him as an opening of loving arms in a welcoming embrace touches a wayworn
and discouraged traveller. For many succeeding days he dwelt on

the shore drinking in the infinitely varied monotony of greatness.
He was moved by the thought that there, at last, he stood on the
threshold of the dwelling place of sublime ideas. He made his own
the fleeting beauties of sunrises and sunsets with the avidity of a
thief, with the determination of a buccaneer. He thought nobody
could see in them what he saw, and the snatching before the eyes
of men of profound impressions had for him all the harsh joy of
unlawful conquest. On hazy evenings after watching the last vestige of a rayless fire sink in the violet distances of the sea he would
remain, listening anxiously, through gathering darkness, to the
measured clamour of the surf. He believed that in that presence
the word would come, the word desired, prayed for, invoked; the
word that would give life, that would give shape, to the unborn
longings of his heart. But the weeks passed, wearing out the
poignant delight of his hope. The great, the unreserved, the illimitable had a reserve and a limit for him; and after speaking for a
while in tones of thunder, fell into an austere and impenetrable silence. He waited—patiently, humbly. At last with a sigh of: "Not
here! Not here!" he turned his back upon the capricious sea.

He felt sad, cast down, unsecure; as a man betrayed by the most
loved of friends would feel. He began to mistrust the whole creation—and naturally he thought of the undesirable security of perfect solitude. He dreamed of vast deserts, but—apart from the
difficulty of living there—he had a fear of their deception. They
also would speak in glorious promises only to cast him down at
last from the pinnacle of his expectations. He would not expose
himself again to a trial almost too heavy to be borne, to a disap-
pointment that would—perhaps—forever rob him of the last vestiges of his faith. Cold silence, absolute silence, is better than the
unfinished melodies of deceived hopes. He resolved to return to
the cities, amongst men; not because of what the poet said about
solitude in a crowd;[5] but from an inward sense of his difference
from the majority of mankind. He would withdraw into the repug-
nance he inspired to men and live there unembittered and pacific.
He liked them well enough. Many of them he liked very much, but
he never felt the sense of his own quality (whatever it might be—
he did not in any way think himself superior—only different) as

when in contact with the latent hostility of his kind. He made up his mind to try Paris—and started at once.

IV

He had visited that town before, in the second year of his travels, and then had, for some months, camped in the land of Bohemia; in that strange holy land of art abandoned by its High Priests; in the land of true faith and sincere blasphemies; where, in the midst of strife for immortal truth, hollow idols sit in imbecile and hieratic poses looking with approving eyes and their tongues in their cheeks at the agitated crowds of neophytes bringing fuel to the undying blaze of the sacred fire. It is a land of dazzling clearness and of distorted shadows; a country loud with the brazen trumpetings of assertion, and eloquent with the whisper of honest hopes and high endeavours; with the sighs of the, not less noble, failures; of not ignoble discouragements. Over it, the mephitic smoke of the sacred fire hangs thick; and the outer world looks with disapproval at the black and repulsive pall hiding the light, the faith, the sacrifices: sacrifices of youth, of burnt hearts, of many bright futures—of not a few convictions!

Stephen would not cross again the frontier of Bohemia. Not having been able to find in achievement the justification of his nebulous desires, he thought himself in all innocence unworthy to associate intimately with those men of so much more distinct aspirations. He had no friends there; did not care to try for friendships; feared to recommence again the weary round of misunderstandings ending in distaste. If any came to him they would be welcome. Meantime he would remain outside and wait. Nobody came. For months he lived alone; working a little, trying to find form before he had mastered the idea, listening to inward voices. A life ineffectual, joyless and tranquil.

He had found on the outskirts of Passy an almost ideal retreat. It was a pavilion in the court of a modern house that brought its shabby façade into line with the sordid range of the street. The pavilion, a much older structure, probably a remnant of a much more dignified building, had a ground floor and only one floor above. On the ground floor there were three rooms in which Stephen lived. A broad stone staircase gave access above to a large room extending over the three under it. It looked like a ballroom exiled from more splendid regions, and its windows, seven of them, overlooked a triangular vestige of some garden— once spacious—now only large enough to accommodate three or four trees, that lived there—as if in a dungeon—between the high blind walls of neighbouring houses. Their pale foliage waved below the windows of the pavilion in a shimmer of green tints that seemed pale and delicate with the pathetic frailness of town children. The sunshine lay on their branches, penetrated no lower, entered the studio as if guessing of the vision of light and colour that unrolled itself there in the head of the restless and solitary man. Below in the damp and uniform gloom the grass sprang up, vigorous and conquering, over that desolate remnant of beauty; covering the ground thickly with a prosperous, flourishing growth in a triumph of undistinguishably similar blades that pressed thick, low, full of life around the foot of soaring trunks of the trees; the grass unconquerable, content with the gloom, disputing sustenance with the roots, vanquishing the slender trees that strove courageously even there to keep their heads in the splendour of sunshine. In the branches a colony of blackbirds—probably unconventional—who had been expelled from ordered communities of the gardens of La Muette led a disorderly, noisy, fluttering, whistling kind of life; flying constantly across the windows in and out of their grimy and disreputable nests; and wondering, perhaps with compassion, at the big stone cage where dwelt an immense and unfortunate creature that could not fly, or whistle, or sing.

On the courtyard side the big room had only two windows; big windows from ceiling to floor, having a wrought-iron guard that rose in a complicated design of arabesque to the height of a man's elbow. The court itself was gravel, with stone walks, right and left along the wings of the main house. In the middle of it a circular clump of flowering bushes, once upon a time ornamental and kept under the control of a stone border, had run wild and luxuriated now in incult freedom. Through the high main building a wide archway, a carriage archway, led into the street. Trailing under the archway, over the court; rising as high as the windows of Stephen's studio, a strong perfume of oranges carried amongst brick walls and over sooty bushes a romantic suggestion of dark foliage and golden fruit, of tepid breezes and clear sunshine, of

rustling groves in a southern land. Outside, the street rattled, murmured, shouted: inharmonious and busy. Inside, the sweet-
scented silence was almost undisturbed by the feeble tapping of
Ortega's hammer. Now and then, about once a week, a heavy van
would stop before the archway and boxes of oranges streamed
into the court on the backs of men that ran in, bent nearly double,
and dumped their loads down with a low groan. Then Ortega's
voice piped all day, thinly voluble, agitated and important. At
times it would be drowned by the harsh tones of strident scolding
under the recess of the archway. The noise would burst violently,
rasp the air with the cruel sharpness of its spite, and in scornful
exclamations drawling crescendo: "They will ruin you under your
nose! Look at that man, José. You see nothing! I will teach him!
But look! Look! All these oranges. . . . Sanctissima . . . Look!
You! José!" Old Ortega, unshaven and dirty, tripped about on his
meagre shanks here and there like a man in extreme distress. And
when the scolding had abruptly ceased his thin squeaky voice
would be heard modulated and persuasive with tender intona-
tions: "But Dolores! . . . Don't! . . . Don't Dolocita! . . . My
dearest!"

V

Those Ortegas were the owners of the house, or rather the man
owned the house which the woman ruled with a perpetually irritated masterfulness. They had established themselves there some
years ago; and the blue signboard over the ground-floor windows,
proclaiming that I. Ortega sold within oranges, olives and wine in
a wholesale way, had become faded with the rains of many au-
tumns before Stephen found rest in the interior pavilion after his
long wanderings. The couple were well-to-do. José, one of the
three children of prosperous Biscayan cultivators, had wandered
away early, seeking martial distinction in the ranks of colonial
troops. Returning, he found for himself in Seville a wife, and then
after many changes had found also what to him seemed, and indeed was, a fortune in commerce far from his native land. His
brother, the genius of the family, had become a priest and now
was in charge of a hamlet full of fiery Basque souls which he en-
deavoured to keep in the path of godliness with fierce denunci-
ations, with menacing words, with gloomy fanaticism, knowing

nothing of the world; hating it, for it was the hospitable playground of the devil, hardly able to bring himself to tolerate the impious sunshine that, by an inexplicable oversight of the Creator, shone indiscriminately upon the believing and upon the wicked. A tall, lean priest with a narrow forehead and an ascetic yet coarse face; moving amongst hot-headed and fearless men, respected, admired and feared wherever he went, indefatigable and keen in his shabby, black, close-fitting cassock, amongst those reckless sinners; ready to leap, for the defeat of evil and error, out of his ominous and concentrated silence, like a sword from the scabbard in the hand of an unforgiving God. A mystical fanatic who in the darkness of black nights saw visions, who in the silence of barren hills heard voices; who living amongst simple men and women felt clearly that he was living in a world inhabited by damned souls. A man of great faith who battled for his belief in an obscure and arid valley of the Pyrenees, wearing out his unyielding heart with the rage, the humiliation, the bitterness of his inefficiency in that terrible contest against the victorious Destroyer of mankind.

The youngest of the three children, a girl, married a mountaineer possessor of a patch of ground and of a ruinous stone dwelling that stood in the unproductive disorder of a narrow valley bestrewn with grey boulders. The fellow, handsome, sinewy and brown-faced, went through life singing: a royalist, a smuggler and a gay companion, very popular amongst the men of the hills, who were ready any day to die for their King and their *fueros*. One evening he went away singing, carbine in hand, into the purple confusion of towering peaks—and never returned. Doubtless he died in good company. And even in these peaceful times the frontier guards talk to this day of that sharp and bloody affair in the pass, where a wooden cross stretches its black arms in stiff indifference, over the common grave of the breakers and the guardians of the law.

The widow, always delicate, sickened seriously soon after. The priest brother came, confessed, absolved, buried her—and took the orphans: two girls.

The priest was poor—very poor. Poor with his own poverty and with all the indigence of his flock. That he was wealthy enough to

endow both girls with the Everlasting Treasure, he never doubted.
Yet he suffered to see them exposed to those privations which for
himself he considered to be a reward too splendid for his merits.
He corresponded irregularly with his brother José—with that
righteous man, amassing wealth, away there in the magnificent
and sinful city. He wrote him of his difficulties. He got an answer
written by his sister-in-law. The virtuous Dolores said her husband had consulted her. Well, as to money, commerce had its ex-
igencies and money was scarce. But they were childless. They
would take one of the girls, care tenderly for her, and, eventually,
marry her to a man of good repute—if Heaven so willed. José on
his annual business tour to Murcia would on his return call on his
brother and take the child. She, Dolores, would be a mother to a
deserving and obedient girl. And the child would have many ad-
vantages. They knew many good people. . . . Father Ortega read
on for four pages, with a thoughtful face, at last with a frown. He
had doubts. On the other hand he trusted his brother. He believed
in the wickedness of mankind with all the innocence of his soul.
With equal innocence he believed in the virtue of Ortegas. In the
appalling desert of human sinfulness the blood of his race flowed
pure like a miraculous stream. José had been a soldier. What of
that! There had been soldiers who also had been saints. José, if no
saint, would be a good Christian. His own brother! Yes! One of
the little ones must go. She also was an Ortega. His parentage was
a safeguard for the child. He could not believe in the possibility of
any of his kin falling away from grace. He would not even think
of it. It would be too terrible.

The brothers met after many years. Away from his "Dolcita, my
dearest!" José bore himself with a free joviality, becoming a successful merchant who had not quite forgotten his warlike youth.
They talked together of old times, of the dead, of the old people,
of the sister they had loved much. Before the stern soldier of the
Faith the ex-sergeant of colonial troops was like a child: affectionate and respectful—a little awed. Father Ortega asked about
the King—the rightful King—who also lived in Paris. Had José
seen him? Yes? Good! A better time was coming. With the rightful
monarch the fear of God would reign in the land. The time would

come! And Father Ortega grew animated, talked loud. The two little girls, standing close together, very quiet, listened open-eyed. As the time for separation approached the priest became tender, very solemn too. "Mind, José," he said impressively, "I deliver to your care a Christian soul. See that you do your duty. A sacred charge!" Poor José was touched and not a little discomposed. He repeated: "Good! Good! Of course! How else?"—and looked down at his imposing charge. He saw only a barelegged girl of about twelve with tumbled brown hair and large grey eyes that streamed with tears. The other one was crying too. He felt moved to tears himself. "Brother," he blubbered out, "I will take . . . take . . . both of them . . . Poor . . . things. Dolcita won't mind!" But the priest refused with an air both exalted and austere. Theresa must remain under his influence. That child had dispositions . . . a sacred spark that must be nursed into a flame. Later on, if there was need for a little money to help her into a convent of her choice, he would ask his brother. She was different from the younger, Rita. She had a vocation—a sacred spark. As he spoke his sunken eyes glimmered, like a pair of votive candles before a rude altar, in the gloom of a wayside shrine.

The sisters parted in the dust of a narrow road that winds along the bottom of the shallow and rocky valley. The brothers clasped each other in a long embrace, then the younger gave his blessing to the elder man, who stood with bared head before the uplifted hand. José and Rita had to walk some little distance to the village where José's conveyance awaited him. Father Ortega, holding Theresa by the hand, turned his back upon the setting sun and stood looking at them as they went on, diminishing in the distance, under the escarpment of the stony cliffs. The priest's shadow fell slender and long on the white dust of the path as if darting after the departing figures; and the shorter shadow of the child, pressing to his side, mingled with it for a part of its length. The two made as though only one distorted and blank image of a giant hound, pointing with a fantastically elongated finger at the young wanderer going into the unknown. The priest stood silent, the child sobbed gently by his side; and they remained gazing till José and Rita disappeared on a turn of the path behind a big detached bush-crowned aslant, with a solitary pine waving on its

summit: a round, grey boulder that lay on the brown flatness of
the sward like an enormous and aged head under a sombre and
plumed béret.

VI

José loved the child. The girl was affectionate in an independent
kind of way, and the old man wanted some unchecked outlet for
the kindness of his heart. She reminded him also of his sister,
whom in having left his home early he remembered best as just
such another girl. To Dolores her husband's niece was interesting
principally as a costly memorial of an unheard-of concession to
conjugal weakness: a concession that must be repaid to her by
years of meek obedience. She was a strange product of ignorance
and shopkeeping instincts. She was the daughter of a man looked
upon in his native town as imbued with Western ideas,[6] a man
very clever and audacious. In fact the only really enterprising ship
chandler of poetical Seville. She could read, even in French, with
assurance—she could write with, not an altogether fatal, hesitation—she could cast up sums, in addition, in her husband's books
with the ease of natural aptitude revelling in a charming occupation. She was prejudiced, unforgiving and knew how best to assert
her personality against José. The gentle combatant of the glorious
Philippine wars, accustomed to discipline of a sort, was not a very
rebellious subject. Still, there were points on which he dared to
have his will—sometimes, even, his way. But with the arrival of
Rita even the shadow of imperfect freedom departed from him.
The astute Dolores soon noticed the strength of his affection for
the child, and from that time Rita's comfort, education, her needs,
her welfare became in Dolores's hand so many irresistible instru-
ments serving to grind José into very small dust. To the consideration of the child's happiness he gave up his tastes, his opinions,
his comforts—even his habits; all—but one! Abnegation has
limits. To save Rita from unjust scoldings, from unnecessary slap-
pings, from being shut up cruelly in a dark room or unnecessarily
deprived of her supper, he would give up his plans of business, his
yearly journeys (those green oases of his life), would consent to
have his opinion on wine or olives impugned, sneered at, over-
ruled; but he would not give up his evening visits to a café where

his countrymen used to congregate. Dolores, with the prudence of an accomplished tyrant, gave way on that point: for a man must not be robbed of every incentive to endure the burden of existence if he is to remain a fit subject for autocratic rule.

Every evening in the festive glare of gaslights, amongst the polish of tall mirrors, the gleam of gildings, the cheerfulness of white marble tables intensified by the glowing, rich note of colour in the crimson plush of the seats, José luxuriated at his ease, enjoying his short-lived liberty, his fleeting sense of self-respect, in the midst of men who would listen, without unkind remarks, to what he had to say. He was an extreme, a ferocious Legitimist, ready, theoretically, to pay the price of war, famine and conflagration for the triumph of his ideas. The sonorous periods of his speech rang with the words extolling "our mother the Holy Church" and the "Rey neto"[7] in strange rhapsodies; while the aproned waiters circulated in the smoke and murmur of the café, clattering with the saucers, beer glasses and coffee cups which they distributed smartly upon crowded tables with an air of bored disdain. José was happy every evening—and all day (more fortunate in that than most men) he had the certitude of that happiness to help him through his trials. It may be said without exaggeration that he lived only for the joy of these moments and—more unselfishly—to watch over Rita.

It is hard to say what the wild girl of Basque mountains, transplanted into the heavy-scented but sordid atmosphere of the house in Passy, would have become had it not been that José found a good friend for the child in one of his café acquaintances of the same political way of thinking with himself. Señor Malagon was socially superior to the seller of oranges, being a considerable leather merchant from Cordova. His circle of acquaintance was extensive, for his wife was French and they moved in a very respectable, well-to-do and proper world of solvent businessmen possessing sociable wives. Mrs. Malagon, a vivacious and sentimental person, was immensely interested in Rita's story as told her by her husband. Poor José wearied all his friends with the eulogies of his niece. Malagon, a grave man with a cameo profile and a bluish chin, listened patiently, raising, from time to time, towards his lips, a beringed hand holding a cigar. José confided to

him his difficulties in hints, in half-admissions of his wife's imprac-
ticability. He spoke, discreet, longing for advice, mindful of his
out-of-doors dignity but ready to sacrifice even that for the good
of his niece. Señor Malagon—imperturbable—heard, pondered
for a long time: impenetrably sympathetic, cautiously dumb. But
the little Mrs. Malagon would not admit any caution. They must
befriend the girl. The daughter of a smuggler killed in the exercise
of his functions? How wicked and romantic! And an orphan?
How sad! Brought up by a solitary priest in a lonely valley? It
made her shiver, but in that case there could be nothing wrong
there. "We must help your friend about her, Henry," she said.
"He is not my friend," protested Henry; "he's just a right-thinking
and respectable Spaniard with whom I played dominoes every
evening for the last year or two. That's all." "And the girl is
pretty?" asked the wife. The husband admitted she was. Strange
but pretty. He had called on Ortega and saw her there. "Business,
you know, my dear," he explained. "Could one speak to that horrid Mrs. Ortega? Could one really venture to go and see her?"
wondered Mrs. Malagon. "H'm! She is very . . . proper. Common
but . . . respectable," admitted Henry, with deliberate heaviness
of diction. He did not want to commit himself to anything very
precise. Personally he had no objection. It did not seem very necessary. Those people were by no means poor. Not at all. Well off,
rather. Still, if his wife liked . . . Malagon, married late in life,
spoiled his wife—paternally.

In this way, after many preliminary manoeuvres of cunning di-
plomacy on the part of José, it came to pass that Mrs. Malagon's
serviceable, one-horse landau was seen at last, waiting before the
wide archway of the Passy house. It cannot be said that Dolores
was very gracious. She could no more smile graciously than a
cockatoo; a bird she resembled somewhat, when viewed from one
side, by the irritated curve of her nose and by the invarying cold
fury of her round and pitiless eye. But she was decently polite and
made no vehement objection to Mrs. Malagon's desires. She only
remarked afterwards that the little Frenchwoman was a fool—to
which opinion the unprincipled José hastened to assent. Of course
she would not part altogether with the child. Indeed it was not
demanded of her. She had no objection, however, to be relieved
now and then from the bother of looking after the girl. "Unruly

minx! Well, if your sister was like that, I am glad I never knew her." José, pretending not to hear, would slink out, to swear and stamp with rage in some secluded place. From sheer affection for Rita he was reduced to a pass where he dared not protest against any abuse, any insult, any blasphemy. He was afraid of what his wife might do. She was capable of going to these people, of abusing them foully, of taking away the child, of making an awful disturbance. She would break the windows perhaps! *Quién sabe?*

VII

Rita, tamed under the heavy hand of Dolores, was softened by the peaceful influences of a commonplace and happy home. The ordered life, the decencies of a civilized household of pretty surroundings—for Mrs. Malagon piqued herself on being cultivated and artistic—seemed to make round her a sort of tender half-light in which the child moved happy, joyous, herself the brightest spot in the haziness of a mediocre daylight, where life appeared a quiet and an easy achievement. Adéle Malagon—only a year younger than Rita—had for her companion that kind of fierce friendship of which only very young girls seem capable. They were very much together, almost continuously, being at first educated together by Miss Malagon's governess. Only now and then Dolores's capricious fiat—when José had to be punished for some want of pliability—would call the girl back into the atmosphere of scolding and garlic of her aunt's home; where, for a few days, or even a couple of weeks, she lived—painfully on the alert; combative and unrestful; prepared for strife, like a warrior in the presence of an enemy. Then her uncle was childishly happy and ludicrously miserable. He admired her bravery in holding out—with more or less success—against Dolores, he enjoyed her caressing ways—that were for him only—and he deplored the state of affairs that hardened the character of the girl. In the other household Adéle moped, the governess—good soul—complained dolefully, "That child will forget everything! When she gets back from that awful house she is positively wicked for a time. I can't manage her." Mrs. Malagon, staring hard with those unseeing, swimming eyes of hers, would murmur serenely, "Oh! It will be all right." At the family luncheon the corpulent Henry would miss the girl and

remark in his profound murmur, "Ho! The little savage gone
again!" And when she returned he greeted her with "Ho! You
have come back? *Bueno!*" Then he complained with ponderous
playfulness about his Adéle learning "that barbarous jargon of
those Biscayans from our wild mountaineer" and distributed im-
partially wholesome bonbons to both children. After dinner, before going to his café, he would sit in his wife's salon wheezing
comfortably and beam in amused silence upon his wife, his Adéle
and that waif of the mountains as if all three were his promising
daughters. In the café José kept his seat, would jump up to meet
him, would shake both his hands at parting. He liked the unassuming old fellow whose opinions were so very sound. Very
sound! From time to time—very seldom—old Ortega, freshly
shaved, scrupulously got up in black—as if he were going to a
funeral—would call on Mrs. Malagon and, after anxious inquiries
if there were no visitors, would be introduced by a pert *bonne* into
the splendour of Mrs. Malagon's knickknacks. Rita's benefactress
—as he called her—received him always with sweet patience
which he did not abuse. His calls were short. To him she appeared
a princess, a queen, nay, more, almost supernatural: a benevolent
fairy that had saved Rita from vague but immense misfortunes.
He stammered, always embarrassed, his heart full, "You are an
Angel. An old man thanks you—with his heart, all his heart!"
When Mrs. Malagon said that it really was a small matter, she was
pleased to do anything for Rita—who was charming; "We all love
her," José would exclaim in a trembling voice: "Isn't she! Who
wouldn't love her? But Heaven has sent you for my comfort. I
kiss your hands and feet."[8] And he always did kiss the little
woman's hands devoutly before going out of that magnificent
drawing room. Mrs. Malagon—when the door had closed after
the simple old fellow—would hold up close to her shortsighted
eyes the plump white hand and look for a time with a faint smile
at a tear José often left there, before she would dry it with quick,
gentle taps of her cambric handkerchief, while she thought, "Am I
really so very good? How extremely touching!"

The peaceful conventions of middle life, the conventions resem-
bling virtues, made for Rita as if a shelter behind a respectable
curtain that separated her from the real existence of passions. The

pretty assumptions of selfish quietude gave to events an aspect of general benevolence, a polished surface of easy curves hiding the resounding emptiness of thoughts, the deadly fear of sincerity, the cherished unreality of emotions. It went on as a tale made up of charming but meaningless sentences, flowing with gentle ease through a succession of serene days. In the shallow stream Rita was carried away from year to year; listened to the soothing imbecility of its babble. Listening, she was willing to forget the impressions of young days, the rugged landscapes, the rugged men, the strong beliefs, the strong passions. To her all this was hardly a matter of experience. It was more like the memory of an atmosphere, the memory of some subtle quality of air made up of freshness of perfumes, of brilliance, of stimulating gusts, of gentle breezes—things intangible, indescribable, not understood; impossible to define and impossible to forget. She thought of them with love, with longing—sometimes with repulsion, often with scorn—now and then with rare lucidity that suggested fear, that swift fear of the unavoidable approaching in dreams. She would shake it off with the smile of unbelief—with the callous innocence that ignores the trammels of its origin. She was so adaptive that her adaptiveness had the aspect of a cruel absence of the heart. She appeared gracious and heartless living in aimless periods of sunshine, living between sunrises and sunsets as if there had been, suspended over her head, no menace of another day.

Only from time to time during her repeated visits to Passy she caught a glimpse of sincere emotions. José's increasing love for herself, the love inarticulate and profound; that unchecked flow of tender impulse relieving the ignorant and oppressed heart was the first thing that struck her as unquestionable and imposing in its absolute openness, in its convincing unreserve. Its helplessness was touching and it seemed to her to be an indissoluble part of it, filling her with regret at the thought that so much affection must be bound up together with so much weakness. Was it always so? Was it always the most sincere that were the weakest? For her uncle as she grew up, she had a caressing, a deep gratitude—in which, almost unknown to her, lurked a faint flavour of disenchanted pity. The vagaries of Dolores she met with a rigidity of demeanour which caused that worthy woman to foam at the

mouth in the imperfect privacy of a big glass cage where she sat
from morning to night with her yellow profile of a bilious parrot
hovering over the pages of account books. The angry miserliness
of Dolores grew with age, rising by its vastness, its stupidity, by
the blind ruthlessness of its strength to the dignity of an elemental
force of nature. And the increasing griminess of the home where
the plaster peeled in slabs between the grey sashes of dusty windows, the leprous aspect of its façade, remarkable even in the
unhealthy blotchiness of the soiled street, hid the cold emptiness
of big rooms: four stories of vast and dirty desolation, through
which, shaking his head dolefully, José shuffled with slippered feet
in futile rounds of mournful and useless inspection.

Notes *to* The Sisters

1. I.e., Cossack; Conrad used here the Polish spelling (*Kozak*).
2. In Polish: *wszystko można, lecz z ostrożna;* similarly in Russian:
mozhno—no ostorozhno.
3. Inn, tavern (Russian).
4. A Polish proverb: *Popie oczy, wilcze gardło, co zobaczy, to by zżarło.*
5. The allusion is to *Childe Harold's Pilgrimage,* canto II, stanzas 25–26:
    To sit on rocks, to muse o'er flood and fell,
    To slowly trace the forest's shady scene,
    Where things that own not man's dominion dwell,
    And mortal foot hath ne'er or rarely been;
    To climb the trackless mountain all unseen,
    With the wild flock that never needs a fold;
    Alone o'er steeps and foaming falls to lean;
    This is not solitude; 'tis but to hold
    Converse with Nature's charms, and view her stores unroll'd.
    But midst the crowd, the hum, the shock of men,
    To hear, to see, to feel, and to possess,
    And roam along, the world's tired denizen,
    With none who bless us, none whom we can bless; . . .
    This is to be alone; this, this is solitude!
We find many other analogies with *The Sisters* in Byron's poem: parting
with parents, canto I—Farewell; weary with life, canto I, stanzas 4–5; lack
of friends, I, 8–9; cult of Nature, II, 48, II, 87, III, 13; difference from the
crowd, III, 113; independence of spirit, II, 12. Possibly Conrad had *Childe
Harold's Pilgrimage* fresh in his mind.
    I thank Professor Charles Hagelman for his suggestion to look into
Byron's poem.
6. An odd phrase, as west of Spain are Portugal and the Atlantic.
7. The true King (Spanish).
8. A traditional, old-fashioned Polish expression.

Conrad's letter to the New York *Times* Saturday Book Review is his only public reply to a criticism, but the interest of the piece lies primarily in the fact that it is also, apart from his Preface to *The Nigger of the "Narcissus,"* the only pronouncement of his views on art and its relation to science.

The letter was occasioned by an unsigned short review of *The Inheritors,* a novel written by Conrad in collaboration with Ford Madox Ford (at that time still F. M. Hueffer), published in the New York *Times Saturday Book Review* on 13 July 1901. The first part of the letter stresses the importance of Ford's share in the work, a share completely ignored by the reviewer. It is amusing to read these expostulations of "the elder of the authors" if one remembers Ford's later patronizing statements on his collaboration with Conrad.[1] Since Conrad's share in writing *The Inheritors* was minuscule, and the novel, in spite of a few good passages, is the worst book he ever put his name on, perhaps it was not only loyalty to the younger co-author but also reluctance to be judged by this lopsided product which prompted him to write the letter. True, the reviewer did not quite get the meaning of the story, but Conrad had been misunderstood in much grosser ways— and kept silent.[2] Perhaps, as an Englishman by choice and in aspirations, he felt stung by the claim that the novel was directed against some "cherished English traditions." Although *The Inheritors* is a satire on contemporary Englishmen, it is not, indeed, an attack on their traditions—rather the contrary. Still, Conrad protests too much, literally, when he says that the book "does not attack personalities." Thinly veiled caricatures of Chamberlain, Leopold II of Belgium, and Northcliffe give the novel whatever liveliness and topicality it possesses.

The last and most interesting part of the letter has nothing to do with *The Inheritors*. Four years after his Preface to *The*

Nigger Conrad again takes up the problem of truth in science and in art. Although he now assigns to art a more passive and limited role, he still thinks that the artist is capable of attaining truth by sheer "fidelity to his sensations." Conrad's discourse on the lack of any absolute principle underlying life and morality and on the irremediable contradiction between egoism and altruism, and then his image of the writer as a "self-less" renderer of the "irreconcilable antagonisms," foreshadow the often-quoted passage in *A Personal Record:* "The ethical view of the universe involves us at last in so many cruel and absurd contradictions, where the last vestiges of faith, hope, charity, and even of reason itself, seem ready to perish, that I have come to suspect that the aim of creation cannot be ethical at all. [. . .] And the unwearied self-forgetful attention to every phase of the living universe reflected in our consciousness may be our appointed task on this earth."[3]

When we look for analogies in philosophy, William James's essay "The Sentiment of Rationality" comes to mind. James presents there his views on "the radical question of life—the question whether this be at bottom a moral or an unmoral universe."[4] Conrad, as we hear from Galsworthy, knew and liked the work of Henry's elder brother.[5] It is virtually certain that he read the then most famous of James's books, *The Will To Believe* (1897), which incorporates the quoted essay. Questions of influence apart, James's view that the contest between materialism and moralism will be settled only when "the experience of the entire human race is taken into account" but that we, in our every act, influence its outcome— seems to be close to Conrad's own sentiment, to his particular blend of skepticism and insistence on moral responsibility.

As in *The Nigger* Preface, art is contrasted here with science, and in a similar way, albeit Conrad's tone is now more austere. These few sentences on the nature of scientific truth should make those who consider Conrad primarily a Schopenhauerian think again. Although it is impossible to pin down unequivocally his philosophical allegiance, it is fairly clear that he was much closer to Avenarius and Mach with their theory of pure sensations as the rock-bed of all knowledge, and to Boutroux's view that scientific theories are hypothetical and contingent constructs not based on a necessary connection of phenomena, than to Schopenhauer's doctrine that the world is *my* willed idea. Nor was Conrad, like Schopenhauer, a monist: the division into natural world and spiritual consciousness was strongly imprinted in his mind. As his agnosticism seems to have owed something to Spencer, we may say that the positivistic philosopher-critics of science prepared him well for his future friendship with Bertrand Russell.

Notes

1. *Joseph Conrad: A Personal Remembrance,* Little, Brown, Boston, 1924, p. 16; *Return to Yesterday,* Gollancz, London, 1931, pp. 186, 192, 207.
2. E.g., I. Zangwill complained in the respectable *Academy* that the material of *The Nigger* "is barely enough for half the number of pages," and the *Illustrated London News* thought the heroes of this novel "are generally worthless personages." See J. D. Gordan, *Joseph Conrad: the Making of a Novelist,* Harvard University Press, Cambridge, Mass., 1940, pp. 269–97; *Conrad: the Critical Heritage,* ed. Norman Sherry, Routledge and Kegan Paul, London and Boston, 1973, pp. 47–128. When Arthur Symons announced (*Saturday Review,* 29 Jan. 1898) that Kipling's *Captains Courageous* and Conrad's *Nigger* had no "idea" behind them, Conrad wrote a reply in form of an article for the *Outlook,* which was, however, never printed.
3. *A Personal Record,* Collected Edition, Dent, p. 92.
4. W. James, *Selected Papers on Philosophy,* Everyman's Library, p. 158.
5. J. Galsworthy, *Castles in Spain and Other Screeds,* Scribner's, New York, 1927, p. 121.

Letter to the New York *Times* Saturday Book Review

Referring to the New York *Times* Saturday Review of July 13, 1901, it is impossible not to recognize in the review of one "extravagant story" the high impartiality exercised in estimating a work which, I fear, remains not wholly sympathetic to the critic.

A feeling of regret mingles with gratitude on that account. It is a great good fortune for a writer to be understood; and greater still to feel that he has made his aim perfectly clear. It might have been wished, too, that the fact of collaboration had been made more evident on the face of the notice.[1] The book is emphatically an experiment in collaboration; but only the first paragraph of the review mentions "the authors" in the plural—afterward it seems as if Mr. Conrad alone were credited with the qualities of style and conception detected by the friendly glance of the critic.

The elder of the authors is well aware how much of these generously estimated qualities the book owes to the younger collaborator. Without disclaiming his own share of the praise or evading the blame, the older man is conscious that his scruples in the matter of treatment, however sincere in themselves, may have stood in the way of a very individual talent deferring to him more out of friendship, perhaps, than from conviction; that they may have robbed the book of much freshness and of many flashes of that "private vision" (as our critic calls them) which would have made the story more actual and more convincing.

It is this feeling that gives him the courage to speak about the book—already written, printed, delivered, and cast to the four winds of publicity. Doubtless a novel that wants explaining is a bad novel; but this is only an extravagant story—and it is an experiment. An experiment may bear a certain amount of explanation without confessing itself a failure.

Therefore it may perhaps be permissible to point out that the story is not directed against "some of the most cherished traditions and achievements of Englishmen." It is rather directed at the self-seeking, at the falsehood that had been (to quote the book) "hiding under the words that for ages had spurred men to noble deeds, to self-sacrifice, and to heroism."[2] And, apart from this view, to direct one's little satire at the tradition and the achievements of a race would have been an imbecile futility—something like making a face at the great pyramid. Judge them as we may, the spirit of tradition and the body of achievement are the very spirit and the very body not only of any single race, but of the entire mankind, which, without the vast breadth and colossal form of the past would be resolved into a handful of the dying, struggling feebly in the darkness under an overwhelming multitude of the dead. Thus our Etchingham Granger, when in the solitude that falls upon his soul, he sees the form of the approaching Nemesis, is made to understand that no man is permitted "to throw away with impunity the treasure of his past—the past of his kind—whence springs the promise of his future."[3]

This is the note struck—we hoped with sufficient emphasis—

among the other emotions of the hero. And, besides, we may appeal to the general tone of the book. It is not directed against tradition; still less does it attack personalities. The extravagance of its form is meant to point out forcibly the materialistic exaggeration of individualism, whose unscrupulous efficiency it is the temper of the time to worship.

It points it out simply—and no more; because the business of a work striving to be art is not to teach or to prophesy (as we have been charged, in this side, with attempting), nor yet to pronounce a definite conclusion.

This, the teaching, the conclusions, even to the prophesying, may be safely left to science, which, whatever authority it may claim, is not concerned with truth at all, but with the exact order of such phenomena as fall under the perception of the senses. Its conclusions are quite true enough if they can be made useful to the furtherance of our little schemes to make our earth a little more habitable. The laws it discovers remain certain and immovable for the time of several generations. But in the sphere of an art dealing with a subject matter whose origin and end are alike unknown there is no possible conclusion. The only indisputable truth of life is our ignorance. Besides this there is nothing evident, nothing absolute, nothing uncontradicted; there is no principle, no instinct, no impulse that can stand alone at the beginning of things and look confidently to the end. Egoism, which is the moving force of the world, and altruism, which is its morality, these two contradictory instincts, of which one is so plain and the other so mysterious, cannot serve us unless in the incomprehensible alliance of their irreconcilable antagonism. Each alone would be fatal to our ambition. For, in the hour of undivided triumph, one would make our inheritance too arid to be worth having and the other too sorrowful to own.

Fiction, at the point of development at which it has arrived, demands from the writer a spirit of scrupulous abnegation. The only legitimate basis of creative work lies in the courageous recognition of all the irreconcilable antagonisms that make our life so enigmatic, so burdensome, so fascinating, so dangerous—so full of hope. They exist! And this is the only fundamental truth of fiction. Its recognition must be critical in its nature, inasmuch that in its character it may be joyous, it may be sad; it may be angry with revolt, or submissive in resignation. The mood does not matter. It is only the writer's self-forgetful fidelity to his sensations that matters. But, whatever light he flashes on it, the fundamental truth remains, and it is only in its name that the barren struggle of contradictions assumes the dignity of moral strife going on ceaselessly to a mysterious end—with our consciousness powerless but concerned sitting enthroned like a melancholy parody of eternal wisdom above the dust of the contest.

Joseph Conrad

Pent Farm, Kent, Aug. 2, 1901

Notes to the Letter to the New York Times *Saturday Book Review*

1. Ford Madox Hueffer is mentioned only in bibliographical footnote to the review, and numerous references in the text are all to Conrad's other works.

2. *The Inheritors* (J. Grant, Edinburgh, 1925), pp. 184–85. (". . . to self-sacrifice, to heroism" in the original)

3. A paraphrase of fragment on p. 200: "in this solitude that had descended upon my soul I seemed to see the shape of an approaching Nemezis. It is permitted to no man to break with his past, with the past of his kind, and to throw away the treasure of his future." Conrad apparently changed the text to strengthen his point.

"The Books of My Childhood" is a reply to a poll conducted by *T.P.'s Weekly* in London. It was published there on 9 January 1903 as the nineteenth answer in the survey.

The Books of My Childhood

I don't remember any child's book; I don't think I ever read any; the first book I remember distinctly is Hugo's *Travailleurs de la Mer*,[1] which I read at the age of seven.

But within the last two years I've participated in my son's (age five) course of reading, and I share his tastes—in prose, Grimm and Andersen; in verse, Lear.

[1903]

Note to "The Books of My Childhood"

1. Victor Hugo's *Toilers of the Sea* (1866) is a novel Conrad's father translated while in exile in Russia.

After the Russian Pacific Fleet had been routed by the Japanese in August 1904, the Baltic Fleet under Admiral Rozhestvenski was dispatched to the scene of war. During the night of October 21, when crossing the North Sea, the squadron opened fire on a fleet of British fishing trawlers on the Dogger Bank (apparently taking them for Japanese torpedo boats). One trawler was sunk and two fishermen killed. The Dogger Bank incident caused an enormous outcry in England, and for some time there was a possibility of military conflict with Russia.

Conrad's letter to the Editor of *The Times,* printed on October 26, 1904, was one of many appearing in this daily alone. It is the first public sign of Conrad's interest in international politics, and particularly in the role of Russia. For a long time a self-avowed political pessimist, he was evidently stirred by the prospect of Russia's decline, which would bring new hopes of independence for Poles and other Central European nations. Such a possibility became imaginable as a result of Russia's unsuccessful war with Japan, begun in February 1904, and the ensuing social revolution in the Western territories of the Empire. A few months after this letter, Conrad wrote his longest political essay, "Autocracy and War"; the novels *The Secret Agent* and *Under Western Eyes* followed.

It is worth noting that, vitriolic as he was in his private letters and articles for the press, Conrad showed more restraint when writing about things Russian in his novels and short stories. One of his last works, "The Warrior's Tale," has as the hero a brave and humane Russian officer, Tomassov.

On The North Sea Outrage
To the Editor of *The Times*

Sir, The position of the fishing boats, victims of the outrage on the part of the Russian fleet, is beyond doubt, but the accounts of the courses steered and the manoeuvres—save the mark—of the squadron appear to me confused. The point, however, which I would raise does not depend upon the correctness of the statements published in the Press.

The firing upon the fishing fleet is an outrage no doubt so extraordinary, so amazing, that it passes into the region of fantasy which borders upon the incredible; for it is hard to believe that even the extreme of nervousness would make a man forget the ABC of his profession in a case so obviously simple.

I know nothing about the handling of a fleet, which is a knowledge appertaining to naval officers and to one or two landsmen— writers who apparently have made a speciality of seamanship *en chambre*. But this is not a question of manoeuvring; it is a simple matter of safe navigation upon which any seaman is competent to speak.

After nearly a quarter of a century of sea service in all sorts of craft, upon seas both narrow and wide (and in the North Sea itself), and in command of both sailing and steam ships,[1] the point I would raise is that the mere taking of a squadron through a fishing fleet is such an outrage, from the seaman's point of view, as any act wantonly courting an accident is bound in conscience to be.

A large fishing fleet can be seen at least at a distance of three miles; it is impossible to mistake the nature of its lights: they blaze at one like a town upon the water. It is an effect of multitude perfectly unmistakable, and the proper and seamanlike practice followed both in sailing and steam ships of the merchant service is to go outside such a fleet; at night always, without exception, and in the daytime almost invariably, unless, indeed, a clear way can be seen between the different clusters of boats with their nets down. In that principle of sea conduct I was brought up by men who certainly were not afraid of handling their ships. To act against it except in case of absolute necessity is nothing short of criminal recklessness. Even in broad daylight the taking of one ship through a fishing fleet is a matter of great care and special vigilance.

As I said, I know nothing of handling a fleet. But naval officers are seamen, and, speaking simply as a seaman of some experience, I make bold to say that no commander of a British squadron, on a passage, would, without necessity and when not engaged in warlike operations, take his ships through a fishing fleet at night. He would not do it on the ground of professional skill and common humanity out of regard for the fishermen's lives and property. The thing is not done. In every ship I have been in, and men I know have been in, the distinct standing order is to go outside all fishing fleets. An officer of the watch disregarding it, especially at night, would lay himself open to a severe reproof from his captain. Fishing boats engaged in their avocations are not fully under command; that is why an international agreement has provided them with lights whose meaning is perfectly clear. Neither are they completely stationary; the fleet drifts as a whole, with variations in the drift of individual boats which causes a constant shifting and shuffling, as it were, of the units composing its body. For this reason, the taking of a ship through a fishing fleet is an operation requiring special vigilance, and involving a risk—a risk which is absolutely useless. I see from the Press that Russian officials in St. Petersburg, with a characteristic impudence, charge the fishermen with falsehood (a charge of lying occurs naturally to the Russian mind), and talk airily of collisions; but my contention is that, even if the boats had been sunk and damaged by collision, it would have been no usual accident, but a wanton outrage. Ships have collided with each other and single fishing smacks have been run down by men who have been made to suffer for such an accident. But no lubber upon the seas has ever gone, as far as I know, into the middle of a fishing fleet, sinking and damaging boats. Such a proceeding passes beyond the limits of accident; it is nothing short of a crime. Stupidity can hardly explain it, unless a stupidity of colossal proportions fit to match the size of the Empire that produced those extraordinary naval officers who are supposed by their countrymen to have done that very thing of steaming a whole fleet through boats at work upon their fishing-ground. How this exploit can be reconciled with the fear of Japanese laying floating mines passes my comprehension. The obvious thing would have been to give that illuminated, blazing mob of deadly engines as wide a berth as possible. The whole thing, unless done for fun, is absolutely inconceivable. If the diagrams I have seen are true, it is nothing short of a miracle that a round dozen of the boats had not been sunk.

But, colossal stupidity or inconceivable malevolence, I am heartily thankful that I am not master of a ship homeward bound in the chops of the Channel in the way of the Russian fleet. To be rammed by a cruiser or a battleship of the Second Pacific Squadron, and then to be left to sink or swim upon the wide sea, is not an eviable fate.

Joseph Conrad

October 23 [1904]

Note to "On The North Sea Outrage"

1. Conrad's habitual exaggeration: he commanded only one sailing ship, the 345-ton barque *Otago,* for fourteen months in 1888–89. The nearest he ever got to commanding a steamship was to replace, for a period of no longer than two weeks, the sick captain Koch, commander of a minute (15-ton) river steamboat, *Roi des Belges,* in the Congo, in September 1890.

The short note "My Best Story and Why I Think So" is an introduction to the reprint of "An Outpost of Progress" in a series of "My Best" short stories published by *Grand Magazine*.

It is interesting to observe Conrad's preference for this story (another candidate would presumably be "Youth," since "Heart of Darkness" was too long for the purpose). The claim of having made a disciplined effort to keep this chilling tale within preconceived artistic limits is documented in Conrad's letters to Garnett of July and August 1896.

The note and the story (first published in *Cosmopolis,* June and July 1897) appeared in London in *Grand Magazine,* March 1906.

My Best Story and Why I Think So
[An Outpost of Progress]

This story, for which I confess a preference, was difficult to write, not because of what I had to write, but of what I had firmly made up my mind not to write into it. What I have done is done with. No words, no regrets can atone now for the imperfections that stand there glaring, patent, numerous, and amusing. The story was written some ten years ago. And yet I remember perfectly well the inflexible and solemn resolve not to be led astray by my subject. I aimed at a scrupulous unity of tone, and it seems to me that I have almost attained it there. It is possible that I am deceiving myself, and that I have missed even that qualified success. But the story is endeared to me by the well-remembered severity of discipline and by one or two moments of flattering illusion.

And all this cannot possibly matter anything to the most benevolent soul amongst the readers of stories.

[1906]

We do not know whether it was the *Daily Mail*, where he had serialized two chapters of *The Mirror of the Sea*, which asked Conrad for an article occasioned by the disappearance of *Waratah*, or whether he himself—at that time extremely hard-pressed financially—took the opportunity to do something that would not be too difficult to write. It was published in the *Daily Mail* on 18 September 1909 and never reprinted. Both in its content and tone it belongs to the *Mirror* series.

The Silence of the Sea

Some five years ago—time passes and the sea alone remains unchanged—I had the pleasure of contributing to this very page of the *Daily Mail* a paper on the theme of "overdue" and "missing" ships—a record of feeling remembered in tranquillity, very personal in tone, and illustrated by the instance of a certain narrow escape of my own.[1] It was but a subjective piece of writing, a bit of prose, saved, if saved at all, by its sincerity. No great merit that. No man who has lived for many years with and by the sea, and even in certain measure *for* the sea, could be wilfully false to that character-moulding element and continue to live on in the hope of saving his soul. Yet, true as it was, remorselessly true to the writer's own sensations, the paper was not very instructive; and as to "actuality," in the journalistic sense of that word, it had, I am thankful to say, none at all at that particular time.

This is not to say that there has ever passed a year of this or any other era in which some ships, big or little, have not been posted as "overdue"—posted as "missing." So it was in the begin-

ning, and so it shall be as long as the science and craft of navigation are not lost to the world—or out of the world. Those two
leaden words of doubt and resignation belong to the very realm of
the ocean, which, conquered as it may be to its innermost depths
and most secret recesses by the curiosity and hardihood of untold
generations, is not to be tamed altogether by the ingenuity of in-
ventive mankind.

"Overdue."

Thus, as I have said before, there is no year in which ships are
not posted as "overdue" and given up as "missing." These words
have a perpetual sinister actuality. But it does not often happen
that an "overdue" ship looms large in the eyes of the anxious
world, a ghostly craft growing indistinct in the mist of an uncertain fate, tragic with the freight of hopes and dread.

Many hearts in two hemispheres are straining with intolerable
anxiety for some sight of the steamship *Waratah*.[2] Her looming
form grows more ghostly from hour to hour—though, of course,
"never say die." We on shore should whisper the precept to ourselves, since we may be certain that the responsible men on board
would be acting on it from the first moment of trouble to the very
last moment of existence. But the ship has been overdue now for,
roughly speaking, six weeks. And this is the sort of anxiety that
does not grow stale.

All the world is in possession of the only sea facts which are
certain: the ship left for a short coastwise run along the curve of
the southern seaboard of the African continent; she left her port
of call in threatening weather, which developed quickly into a very
heavy gale from the westward, and therefore generally adverse to
her on all the courses she had to steer while pursuing her way parallel to the contour of the African shore.

And she has been six weeks overdue! The sea does not give up
all its secrets to the prying anxiety of men. The anguish of hearts
is nothing to it. It is not tamed enough to surrender what terrors
have been left to it by the progress of science and the records of
experience, by patient surveys and patent sounding machines, by
the alliance of iron and fire, by the accumulated knowledge of a
multitude of seamen, and by the perfect riveting of water-tight
bulkheads. No. Not tamed enough yet, not sufficiently stripped of
its robe of mystery. Within the rent and tattered folds of the

sombre garment there may lurk yet the form of some inconceivable disaster. But—never say die!

THE FIRST "MISSING" STEAMER.

The first "missing" record in the history of the passenger service
was, I believe, the paddle steamship *President,* bound from England to New York in the early 'forties.[3] She was supposed to have
run full tilt against an iceberg. That is, very likely, the true explanation of her disappearance. She must have gone down like a
stone.

This is one of the dangers of the sea; yet within the recollection
of my seagoing life the steamship *Arizona,* one of the ocean grey-
hounds of the middle 'eighties, repeated the supposed performance of the *President.* There can be no doubt that she *did* run
against an iceberg, because she lived to tell the tale and exhibit
her wonderfully smashed bows. Verily the water-tight bulkhead
has robbed the ocean of some of its terrors. But, considered in
relation to the fate of the *Waratah,* this danger of the sea, peculiar
mainly to the North Atlantic and to the far southern water routes
of the globe, may be dismissed as inconceivable. It *is* inconceivable that a treacherous floe should have come all the way from
the Polar ice-cap to fish for steamers on the African coast—and in
the dead of winter too!

Water-logged wrecks and uncharted rocks are among the dangers of the sea. But water-logged wrecks are only to be found in
the tracks of the timber trade, and are very rare now, because the
corpse of an iron ship, even if stuffed full of planks, generally
manages to sink out of the way of the living in a very short time.
As to rocks, the coast skirted by the *Waratah* is perfectly charted,
if very rocky in many places.

The fog is the most wicked accomplice of all the dangers of the
sea; but we know that there was no fog. There was a gale. What a
seaman would call very heavy weather. Against this were pitted
the seamanlike qualities of the men who manned her and the sea-
worthiness of the ship—product of the science, the skill, the honesty of other men whose hands drafted her lines, put together the
hull and engines, and launched her upon the sea.

ON THE AGULHAS BANK.

In those matters the writer can depend upon the testimony of his senses. One of the dangers of the ocean is the seas. I use that word in the sense of waves, a term which does not come glib to a seaman's tongue and refuses to slip easily under a pen accustomed to record the memories of a time far removed from the modes of thought and speech common to the shore. On the edge of the Agulhas Bank the seas, driven by a westerly gale, are terrible in their steepness. In sailor's phrase, they come at one like a wall. In the month of August of the year 1884 the writer was involved, on the very path which the *Waratah* should have pursued, in a case which missed narrowly being the case of a missing ship. The vessel on board of which he served went on her beam ends and remained lying thus on her side for thirty hours among these steep seas, whose menacing aspect and vicious rush are not be forgotten.[4] It was a long-drawn experience, an agonisingly prolonged opportunity to "never say die." I suppose we never said it (from the habit and tradition of restraint in that professional matter), though we certainly believed that the time had come for us to do that thing which is never to be spoken of as long as one's ship remains afloat.

Yet dangerous in character as the seas can grow when driven by the headlong winds of that part of the world, it is not to be suggested for a moment that they could by their sheer weight and fury ever overwhelm a steamship like the *Waratah* handled by an experienced seaman, not deeply loaded, of the size and build to defy the worst the sea has been known to do. And should she by a most improbable mischance have become disabled in her engine-room at the height of the gale, there are resources in seamanship to meet such a grave eventuality.

THE POSSIBILITY OF COLLISION.

But there is another steamer overdue in the same quarter of the globe; and the mind of a seaman brooding over the fate of ships and the dangers of the sea cannot overlook the possibility of collision.

We have seen lately in the case of a big Atlantic liner that this, the worst danger of the modern sea, is robbed of much of its deadlines by the invention of water-tight bulkheads. Yet more than once both colliding ships have been known to sink at one stroke. And a collision in heavy weather, even if not immediately fatal to either, is bound to put both ships in extreme jeopardy, for no ship thus wounded, and with one or more of her compartments full of water, can face with the buoyant courage of a good sea boat the stress of the gale and the blows of the assaulting seas.

Reluctantly the possibility of this very thing having happened must be faced—the combination of two dangers of the sea. But he who remembers the tales passing from lips to lips in the world of great water, tales of ships lost and found again, all these tales belonging to the tradition of the wonders of the sea, will never say die. Never. At first in hope, afterwards perhaps because men's grave silence is the only dignified answer upon the cruel mysteries of the sea.

And, after all, ships have been lost not only for weeks on this small and stormy world of ours, but for months—whole months strung on end together to the number of three and more. One remembers brave tales, wonderful instances too long to tell of here, but whose moral is that we must never say die.

[1909]

Notes to "The Silence of the Sea"

1. It was published, as "Overdue and Missing," in the *Daily Mail* in the two installments, on 8 March and 16 November 1904.

2. The *Waratah,* a large and new (built in 1908) passenger and cargo ship of 9,339 tons, left Durban on 26 July 1909 with 211 passengers on board and was never seen again. There is no doubt that she capsized in heavy seas on July 28. (K. C. Barnaby, *Some Ship Disasters and Their Causes,* London, 1968, pp. 45–47.)

3. The *President,* a steamship built in 1839 and regarded as the finest ship of the day, left New York (not England, as Conrad says) for Liverpool in March 1841 and disappeared. It is almost certain that she hit an iceberg.

4. Conrad was at that time serving as second mate on the 1,336-ton clipper *Narcissus*. The story of the ship lying on her side is described in his *Nigger of the "Narcissus."*

The Author's Note to the first American edition of *A Set of Six* precedes by five years Conrad's second preface to this volume, written for the collected edition of his works. It sounds oddly businesslike in its apologies and contains a hardly tenable proposition about "a certain unity of mood" of the stories in the *Set of Six* volume.

The Note was printed only once, in the Doubleday edition of *A Set of Six,* New York–Garden City, 1915.

Author's Note
[to the first American edition of *A Set of Six*]

"The Duel," the longest story in this volume, has appeared already some years ago under the title "The Point of Honor" in the form of a small book adorned by a few clever illustrations; but at my urgent request Messrs. Doubleday, Page and Co. have agreed to reprint it in its proper place in the *Set of Six,* under the title it bore in the first English edition.

I don't think there is anything objectionable in this revival. On the contrary. The choice lay between restoring that tale to its proper home and surroundings and the cutting down of the *Set of Six* to a *Set of Five.*

But the *Set of Six,* if not an organic whole, is a homogeneous group written with a certain unity of method. Moreover "The Duel" is, so far, my only attempt at historical fiction: as earnest an attempt as if the work were ten times its size. To see it dropped out of its place in the collection would have been very painful to my parental feelings.

The return of this tale to the light of day has made me happy. The buyers of the volume will obtain a good many more pages for their money—and that surely cannot be made a ground of complaint. Those who have read the tale on its first appearance by itself in the form of a little book can easily skip it in the collection. As to the possessors of the little book, they may draw comfort from the thought that they own something which in time is likely to become a bibliographical curiosity of some value.

The readers who may feel shocked or annoyed at meeting an old acquaintance under another name are begged to accept my apologies. This is entirely my own doing. I have insisted on the reinstatement of the original title as if it were something of extreme importance. Why it should appear so to me I can't explain very well. It is a matter of sentiment in which I have been very kindly humoured by Messrs. Doubleday, Page and Co. It was an amiable weakness on their part which my readers, who I trust are also my friends, will scarcely count them for a crime.

Joseph Conrad

[1915]

To a special edition of his two disparate stories, *Youth* and *Gaspar Ruiz,* published by Dent in 1920, Conrad gave a preface, which consists of two parts of a different origin. The section dealing with "Youth" comes straight from the Author's Note to the volume *Youth and Two Other Stories,* written in 1917. The other section, presenting "Gaspar Ruiz," was written expressly for this preface and differs from the comments on the story which form part of the Author's Note to the *Set of Six* volume (1920).

The piece was never reprinted, and the text given here follows the original edition (J. M. Dent, London and Toronto, n.d.).

From the Preface to "Youth" and "Gaspar Ruiz"

The story "Gaspar Ruiz" is not a piece of personal experience like "Youth." It is truly fiction, by which I do not mean that it is merely invented, but that it is truely imagined from hints of things that have really happened and of people that have really existed at that time, in that locality and under those special conditions of life. It can be easily understood that for that sort of work, which is of course of a creative (not reminiscent) nature, a certain knowledge of the epoch, the outcome of reading and mental assimilation, was necessary. I need not say that such knowledge as I had was used throughout with a scrupulous regard to the truth of it. No incident was introduced arbitrarily but only as a necessary touch in the general picture. In this arrangement consists the art of story telling as distinguished from the style. My suggestion for "Gaspar Ruiz" I found in an old book of travels published in

1830,[1] both as to his personal appearance and to certain facts and adventures of his life. But the real name of the man was Benavides[2] and he was really for a time chief of a band of Partisans during the Independence War in South America, in the years 1822–24. He *did* change sides, his wife *was* betrayed to one of his enemies, as in the story, together with his little girl, and his character really *was* audacious, ruthless and enterprising. He was really visited by the officers of a British man-of-war in reference to the release of some captured Englishmen. But all this information was contained in less than two full pages of the book. I had to imagine the motives of actions, the various states of people's minds, and the outward appearance of all the persons involved in the tale. Yet no incident or trait of character has been introduced for the sake of its mere sensational value, but only in order to give a true presentation of the feelings, perplexities and passions roused in human breasts by a sequence of certain events which, in the strictest truth, might have happened, and for the most part *did* actually happen, at that time and place.

The episode of the gun fired from the man's back is a reminiscence of my boyhood's reading. Much later in life I heard of it again as an undoubted fact. I am assured, that, supposing the gun to be an old brass four-pounder,[3] taking into account the exceptional physique of Gaspar Ruiz and the use of such a comparatively mild explosive as the gunpowder of that time, it is not impossible.

Notes to Preface to Gaspar Ruiz

1.   In his Note to *A Set of Six* Conrad identifies the book as one by Captain Basil Hall. However, he is mistaken in his dates: The book, published in Edinburgh in 1824, bears the title: *Extracts from a Journal written on the coast of Chili, Peru, and Mexico in the years 1820, 1821, 1822.* The relation of "Gaspar Ruiz" to this source is presented in detail by N. Sherry, *Conrad's Western World,* pp. 137–46.

2.   "Benavides" was the title of the story originally, as shown in Conrad's letters to Pinker (e.g., 18 October 1904).

3.   Conrad has evidently forgotten his own description of the weapon as a "seven-pounder field gun" (*A Set of Six,* p. 60).

The cablegram to the Committee of the Polish Government Loan in Washington, D.C., is unique among Conrad's writings, as it is his only cablegram intended for circulation and his only direct appeal for public support of the new Polish state. (His essay "The Crime of Partition," published in 1919, purported to explain to the English reader the circumstances of Poland's fall and reconstruction.) The text, slightly adjusted, was quoted in full in an article by Maurice Francis Egan, "Our Debt to Poland," published in New York's *The Outlook* on 28 July, 1920. Whether it was circulated in any other way is unknown.

Poland was at that time engaged in a war with Soviet Russia, and the Polish state, reborn after over a hundred years of foreign rule, was in an extremely difficult financial situation. It was hoped that the Americans, in memory of the part Poles had taken in their war of national independence, would be willing to help the embattled country. A special appeal was made to Americans of Polish descent. But the success of the loan (bonds were issued at 6 per cent interest, payable in twenty-six years) was limited, especially as the subscription campaign took place while the very survival of independent Poland was in doubt. One day before Conrad dispatched his cablegram, Poles launched an offensive, which on May 7 gave them Kiev. But when the subscription was opened on May 23, the Russians were already starting a powerful counteroffensive, which was stopped only on August 14 on the outskirts of Warsaw. The war ended on October 12 with a total rout of the Soviet Army.

The story of Conrad's cablegram and of the loan itself is told by Alexander Janta: "Conrad's 'famous cablegram' in support of a Polish loan," *The Polish Review* (New York), spring 1972, pp. 69–77. The article contains a reproduction of the original manuscript, now in Mr. Janta's possession.

The autograph bears a note, signed by Conrad: "This is
the draft of message cabled to U.S. at the request of the Pol-
ist Govt. Comm[itt]ee for State Loan." Contrary to Mr.
Janta's statement, the note indicating the date of dispatch is
also in Conrad's hand.

Cablegram to the Committee for the Polish Government Loan, Washington

For Poles the sense of duty and the imperishable feeling of nationality preserved in the hearts and defended by the hands of their
immediate ancestors in open struggles against the might of three
Powers and in indomitable defiance of crushing oppression for
more than a hundred years is sufficient inducement to come forward assist in reconstructing the independence, dignity and use-
fulness of the reborn Republic, investing generously in honour of
the unconquered dead in testimony of their own national faith and
for the peace and happiness of future generations.

To Americans one appeals for the recognition of that patriotism
not of the flesh but of the spirit which has sustained them so well
in the critical hours of their own history, in the name of common
memories at the dawn of their own independent existence, on the
ground of pure humanity, and as to lovers of perseverance and
courage in all its forms. They can't but feel sympathy for an
idealism akin to their own in this example of unselfish union of
all hearts and all hands in the work of reconstruction. For the
only sound ground of Democracy is unselfish toil in a common
cause. They would wish to help in rebuilding that outpost of Western civilization, once overwhelmed[1] by but never surrendered to
the forces representing what they themselves most detest: inhu-
manity, tyranny and moral lawlessness.

Please edit as required. Salutations.

Joseph Conrad

Dispatched on Monday 26 Ap. 1920

Note to the cablegram to the Committee
for the Polish Government Loan

1. An allusion to the partitions of Poland (1772, 1793, 1795) between Russia, Prussia and Austria. See Conrad's "The Crime of Partition," *Notes on Life and Letters.*

In 1921 the Conrads spent over two months on Corsica (they left, by car, on January 23 and came back on April 10), and it is there that they met Miss Alice S. Kinkead, a painter exhibiting since 1897 and specializing in portraits and landscapes. Conrad's introduction to the catalogue of her exhibition is his only piece of writing directly related to the visual arts. He talks mostly about the landscape itself, not about the paintings; and he is understandably evasive in his remarks on Ireland, which he probably never visited.

The text is reproduced from the catalogue, published by The United Arts Gallery, 23a Old Bond Street, London, in November 1921. The exhibition took place in November and December.

Foreword
to
Corsican and Irish Landscapes
[of Alice S. Kinkead]

In this exhibition of landscapes from two islands, of which one has a hold on the very heart of the artist and the other has appealed irresistibly to her artistic perceptions, will be found not alone complete fidelity to the natural features of the land, but also the expression of the inner character of things which demands interpretation, and is, so to speak, personal to the interpreter. The first thing suggested by this collection is that Corsica is not a subject for every painter. After a short visit in the far-off days of boyhood,[1] or revisiting it again this year that vague thought had become an absolute conviction.

No! Corsican landscape is not everybody's subject. It is dangerous by the apparent facility of its Alpine type which, like certain types of very fine faces, lends itself to commonplace, as if it were a mask rather than the envelope of the soul. Nothing could be made more banal by the exercise of mere skill or even by a vision not frankly and delicately personal than snow-crags, tormented rock-faces, fantastic pinnacles bordered by a blue sea. The truth of Corsican landscape is a matter of deeper vision; its features do not impose themselves by mere grandeur of desolation or exceptionality of form—things easy to capture on the canvas. Yet all those things are there! But in this series of pictures something more has been captured, something extremely subtle, composed of amenity and ruggedness which may be felt obscurely by any one, but which this artist, so faithful in her technique, has rendered with imaginative and touching insight. These pictures, so full of light and truth, contain all the wildness and all the transparent suavity, *suavita de aiere,* which give its unique charm to the Corsican landscape.

So much for Corsica. As to the other, her native island, there must be added to her individual and appreciative vision of beauty, as found in the world at large, the deeper sense of pathos born of love, something on which the emotions of a non-native are not perhaps capable of pronouncing a worthy appreciation. An artist who had perceived the inner truth of a foreign landscape by the power of imaginative sympathy could not fail to render still more finely the spirit of her native land shining upon its outward face; to respond more intimately still to the tie of old association, an association going back into the soil, an association that, like all manifestations of inherited personality, is really unanalysable in its profounder appeal.

J.C.

[1921]

Note to "Foreword to Corsican and Irish Landscapes"

1. Apparently Conrad visited Corsica during his years in Marseilles, 1874–78.

Conrad's "The First Thing I Remember" was one of many replies to the poll conducted by *John O'London's Weekly*. His emotional attachment to the memory of his mother finds here one more confirmation, and so does his propensity for making mistakes about his own age.

The First Thing I Remember

I very much doubt whether anybody remembers things that happened when he or she was a baby. One generally is told of them afterwards and then thinks one remembers. For instance, "I remember" that when I was three years old, or perhaps a little less, I had part of a cheek and an ear frost-bitten. I fancy I can remember being rubbed with snow in the approved fashion in the midst of a great concourse and uproar of alarmed people around me; that I, personally, regarded this treatment with extreme indignation as an utterly unprovoked assault on the part of the people concerned, and was afterwards consoled by being given a cup of chocolate to drink, which, apparently, then, was the greatest treat imaginable for me. I have, however, a strong suspicion that I have been only told of all this and that the image-memory is a later fabrication.

The memory of a visual impression may be more trustworthy, and in that sense I think my earliest memory is of my mother at the piano; of being let into a room which to this day seems to me the very largest room which I was ever in, of the music suddenly stopping, and my mother, with her hands on the keyboard, turning her head to look at me. This must have been early in 1861, when I couldn't have been more than two and a half years old.[1] This, I rather think, is a genuine instance of the memory of a moment; for I do not remember who opened the door for me nor yet how I came there at all. But I have a very convincing impression of details, such as the oval of her face, the peculiar suavity of her eyes, and of the sudden silence. That last is the most convincing as to the genuineness of its being an experience; for, as to the rest, I have to this day a photograph of her from that very time, which, of course, might have gone to the making up of the "memory."

[1921]

Note to "The First Thing I Remember"

1. In early 1861 Conrad was over three years old. His days of happy childhood, to which this reminiscence belongs, ended in October of that year.

The appreciative note to an anthology of writings of his younger friend Hugh Walpole (1884–1941) was written during Conrad's sojourn on Corsica in 1921. Walpole was at that time a very popular author of novels, short stories and travel books, dealing chiefly with upper-class English life. He also wrote one of the first book-length studies of Conrad (*Joseph Conrad,* 1916). Walpole was one of Conrad's close friends in the last years of the writer's life.

The note is reprinted from *A Hugh Walpole Anthology,* London, 1922.

A Hugh Walpole Anthology
Introductory Note

This is not the place nor the occasion to enter into a profounder appreciation of Mr. Hugh Walpole's work. An anthology should speak for itself, and the anthology so intelligently compiled, within its limits, in this little book is bound to offer a sample of literary shade for every reader's sympathy. Sophistication is the only shade that does not exist in Mr. Walpole's prose.

Of the general soundness of Mr. Walpole's work I am perfectly convinced. Let no modern and malicious mind take this declaration for a left-handed compliment. Mr. Walpole's soundness is not of conventions but of convictions; and even as to these let no one suppose that Mr. Walpole's convictions are old-fashioned. He is distinctly a man of his time; and it is just because of that modernity, informed by a sane judgment of urgent problems and a wide and deep sympathy with all mankind, that we look forward hopefully to the growth and increased importance of his work. In his style, so level, so consistent, Mr. Hugh Walpole does not seek so much for novel as for individual expressions; and this search, this ambition so natural to an artist, is often rewarded by success. Old and young interest him alike and he treats both with a sure touch and in the kindest manner. I cannot here refer specifically to passages contained in this excellent selection. In each of them we see Mr. Walpole grappling with the truth of things spiritual and material with his characteristic earnestness, and in the whole of them we can discern other characteristics of this acute and sympathetic explorer of human nature: his love of adventure and the serious audacity he brings to the task of recording the changes of human fate and the moments of human emotion, in the quiet backwaters or in the tumultuous open streams of existence.

J.C.

[1921]

Captain J. G. Sutherland was the commander of *H.M.S. Ready,* a brigantine especially equipped to fight German U-boats, on which Conrad spent two weeks in November 1916. The expedition was a part of arrangements made by the British Admiralty to enable Conrad to observe various naval war activities.

The book is overblown and padded, which explains the evasive tone of Conrad's note—an "anti-foreword," one might say.

The text printed follows J. G. Sutherland, *At Sea with Joseph Conrad,* London, 1922. The book contains a few photographs.

Foreword
[to J. G. Sutherland: *At Sea with Joseph Conrad*]

Dear Captain Sutherland,

When you first told me of your intention to publish a little book about the cruise of the *Ready* in October–November 1916, and asked me if I had any objection, I told you that it was not in my power to raise an effective objection, but that in any case the recollection of your kindness during those days when we were shipmates in the North Sea would have prevented me from putting as much as a formal protest in your way. Having taken that attitude, and the book being now ready for publication, I am glad of this opportunity of testifying to my regard for you, for Lieutenant Osborne, R.N.R., and for the naval and civilian crews of H.M. Brigantine *Ready,* not forgetting Mr. Moodie, the sailing master, whose sterling worth we all appreciated so much both as a seaman and as a shipmate.

I have no doubt that your memories are accurate, but as these are exclusively concerned with my person I am at liberty, without giving offence, to confess that I don't think they were worth preserving in print. But that is your affair. What this experience meant to me in its outward sensations and deeper feelings must remain my private possession. I talked to very few persons about it. I certainly never imagined that any account of that cruise would come before the public.

When the proofs of the little book, which you were good enough to send me, arrived here, I was laid up and not in a condition to read anything. Afterwards I refrained on purpose. After all, these are your own recollections, in which you have insisted on giving me a prominent position, and the fitness of them had to be left to your own judgment and to your own expression.

Joseph Conrad

Oswalds. Bishopsbourne.
[1922]

The note on Marcel Proust is Conrad's only extended comment about any major twentieth-century writer.

Proust died on 18 November 1921, and tributes to him were immediately planned by his English admirers. Coincidentally, Conrad was at that time immersed in *À la Recherche du temps perdu*. He wrote to Christopher Sandeman on 21 November: "I've lately read nothing but Marcel Proust."[1] He was first approached, with the view of taking part in a public homage, by J. C. Squire, whom he answered in a letter of November 30. He said that he had heard of Proust eight or nine years before and has been a great admirer of his art. He valued particularly Proust's descriptions of a unique past, and also the fact that his art was based on analysis.[2]

The project Squire wrote about fell through; but Conrad was soon approached again by C. K. Scott-Moncrieff, who was to become the celebrated translator of Proust. He replied in a letter dated 17 December 1922,[3] repeating most of the thoughts expressed earlier in his letter to Squire. The fragment is one of the most original critical pieces which Conrad ever wrote.

"Proust as Creator" follows the text printed originally in *Marcel Proust—An English Tribute,* ed. C. K. Scott-Moncrieff, London, 1923. It contains the main body of Conrad's letter to Scott-Moncrieff, mentioned above.

Notes

1. G. Jean-Aubry, v. II, p. 287.
2. Joseph Conrad, *Listy,* ed. Zdzisław Najder, Warszawa, 1968, pp. 431–32. The original of the letter is in the Library of Indiana University.
3. G. Jean-Aubry, v. II, pp. 290–92.

Proust as Creator

As to Marcel Proust, *créateur,* I don't think he has been written about much in English, and what I have seen of it was rather superficial. I have seen him praised for his "wonderful" pictures of Paris life and provincial life. But that has been done admirably before, for us, either in love, or in hatred, or in mere irony. One critic goes so far as to say that Proust's great art reaches the universal, and that in depicting his own past he reproduces for us the general experience of mankind. But I doubt it. I admire him rather for disclosing a past like nobody else's, for enlarging, as it were, the general experience of mankind by bringing to it something that has not been recorded before. However, all that is not of much importance. The important thing is that whereas before we had analysis allied to creative art, great in poetic conception, in observation, or in style, his is a creative art absolutely based on analysis. It is really more than that. He is a writer who has pushed analysis to the point when it becomes creative. All that crowd of personages in their infinite variety through all the gradations of the social scale are rendered visible to us by the force of analysis alone. I don't say Proust has no gift of description or characterisation; but, to take an example from each end of the scale: Françoise, the devoted servant, and the Baron de Charlus, a consummate portrait—how many descriptive lines have they got to themselves in the whole body of that immense work? Perhaps, counting the lines, half a page each. And yet no intelligent person can doubt for a moment their plastic and coloured existence. One would think that this method (and Proust has no other, because his method is the expression of his temperament) may be carried too far, but as a matter of fact it is never wearisome. There may be here and there amongst those thousands of pages a paragraph that one might think over-subtle, a bit of analysis pushed so far as to vanish into nothingness. But those are very few, and all minor instances. The intellectual pleasure never flags, because one has the feeling that the last word is being said upon a subject much studied, much written about, and of human interest—the last word of its time. Those that have found beauty in Proust's work are perfectly right. It is there. What amazes one is its inexplicable character. In that prose so full of life there is no reverie, no emotion, no marked irony, no warmth of conviction, not even a marked rhythm to charm our ear. It appeals to our sense of wonder and gains our homage by its veiled greatness. I don't think there ever has been in the whole of literature such an example of the power of analysis, and I feel pretty safe in saying that there will never be another.

Joseph Conrad

[1922]

Alec John Dawson (1872–1951) and his brother Ernest (1884–1960) were two of Conrad's friends of long standing. A. J. Dawson was a prolific writer, a traveler and soldier. Conrad's foreword is reproduced from A. J. Dawson, *Britain's Life-boats,* London, 1923.

Foreword to A. J. Dawson: *Britain's Life-boats*

No voluntary organisation for a humane end has the reputation and the prestige of the Royal National Life-boat Institution, a clearer record of efficiency and, one may say, of brotherly devotion. But it is only those who have followed the sea for their livelihood that know with what confidence the Life-boat Service is looked upon by those for whose benefit it has been founded by the generosity of people who live ashore. Myself a British seaman, with something like twenty years' service, I can testify to that feeling, and to the comfort the existence of Life-boat Stations, with their ever ready crews, brings to the hearts of men on board ships of all nations approaching our shores in dangerous weather. I can bear witness to our unshakable belief in the Life-boat organisation and to our pride in the achievements of our fellow seamen, who, husbands and fathers, would go out on a black night without hesitation to dispute our homeless fate with the angry seas. I remember well how affectionately we looked at those white and blue boats of characteristic shape into which (through a slot in the deck) we used to drop a little silver on paying-off days; feeling that we could do but little in that way, but daring to hope that we, too, serving the overseas commerce of this generous country, were not upon the whole unworthy of the assistance given us for the preservation of property under our care and for the saving of our obscure lives.

                                                                 Joseph Conrad

[1923]

On 17 April 1923, four days before leaving on his trip to the United States, Conrad gave a brief congratulatory speech at the ninety-ninth annual meeting of the Lifeboat Institution held at Aeolian Hall in London.

The speech, according to Conrad's own note the first in his life, contains a tribute to the lifeboat service and a couple of warm and characteristically incorrect references to the beginnings of his sea career. As in his other reminiscences, he extols the friendliness of his British seamen-teachers—and, as usual, he confuses chronology and expands the time of his service.

The speech is mentioned in Conrad's letter to Eric Pinker of 9 April 1923, published by Jean-Aubry in *Life and Letters*, II, pp. 302–03. However, the existence of its text has never been mentioned by Conrad's bibliographers.

Two versions of the draft exist, both now at the Beinecke Library, Yale. One, written, titled, and signed in Conrad's hand, was originally presented (or perhaps sold) to Thomas J. Wise, as indicated in a letter to this collector from Conrad's secretary, Miss Hallowes, dated 16 April 1923 (Yale). This holograph draft has been much worked upon, with many words and phrases written in. However, Conrad put it aside without giving it a final check. It contains a few minor errors ("seamens friends ashore") and shows that, after altering an expression, Conrad did not always bother to change the syntax of the whole sentence accordingly (thus left "honoured" instead of "honouring").

The other version is typewritten (a carbon copy), untitled, unsigned, with a few typed-in corrections. It was acquired by Yale from the widow of G. Jean-Aubry. The typed text is free from grammatical inconsistencies and errors, but it does not represent a finally corrected version either. Perhaps

Conrad inspected only the top copy of typescript and did not
look at the carbon copy. This would explain why in the manuscript we have geographically misplaced Pakenham, and in
the typescript a nonexistent Pukefield appears. Therefore,
since neither text can be considered the one definitely approved by its author, I have decided to publish both slightly
different versions of this short speech, leaving all errors and
misspellings uncorrected.

Draft of Speech to Be Made at the Lifeboat Institution at the Ninety-ninth Meeting.
17 April 1923

I feel it a privilege to be called upon to speak in support of the
resolution in honour of life-boat men of to day worthy inheritors
of a hundred year's tradition of devoted service, and recording
our gratitude to seamens friends ashore who for more than three
generations gave their time, their work and their money to the
welfare of this national organisation so universally known and
trusted that a seaman of any nationality directly he has sighted
our shores feels himself the object of its unfailing care.

The first words about our life-boat service I ever heard in my
life (and that was before good many of you in this hall were
born), I mean living words not words in print, were from the lips
of a Breton in seaman in the West Indies. He had been it seems
wrecked on our coast at one time and what he said was: on those
(he meant our men) you can always depend. They won't give you
up.

A great testimony. I know now of my own knowledge that life
boat men may fail sometimes—there is no shame in being
defeated by the sea—but they don't give up.

I am especially gratified that in this particular life saving service, which this meeting is honoured to-day, it is the Lowestoft men
who have not failed.[1] For it is on board a Lowestoft coaster that I
began my life under the merchant flag,[2] the North Sea being my
school and Lowestoft and Pakenham[3] men—six of them[4]—being
my masters for some three months[5]—a full school term one may

say. I can never forget the friendliness the Lowestoft people to a strange youngster. They may have been amused at me but they taught many of a seaman's duties and the very terms of our sea-speech. It is on this ground that I venture to congratulate you personally not so much on the public recognition you have received today at the hands of a great sea officer[6] before the most distinguished company, as on the success of your efforts in saving that steamship's crew who looked to you for their lives with that confidence which is the reward of men who never give up.

(The first speech of my life)

Notes to the Draft of Speech

1. The meeting was especially honoring the crews of the Lowestoft motor lifeboat and the Gorleston pulling and sailing lifeboat, which, in October 1922, after two nights and a day of struggling with a fierce northeasterly gale, rescued the whole crew of twenty-four of the steamship *Hopelyn* of Newcastle. The coxswains of both boats were awarded gold medals.

2. In fact, Conrad began his life under the Red Banner on board the steamship *Mavis,* which he signed on in Marseilles, 24 April 1878. His second British ship was a small coastal schooner, *Skimmer of the Sea,* which he signed on in Lowestoft, 11 July 1878. It was commanded by William Cook of Lowestoft, and two other members of the crew were also from Lowestoft.

3. Pakenham is an island village in Suffolk, near Bury Saint Edmunds. Conrad had Pakefield in mind; the mate of the *Skimmer* and one able-bodied seamen were Pakefield men.

4. The crew consisted of seven men.

5. Conrad served on the *Skimmer* for seventy-three days: 11 July–23 September 1878.

6. Admiral of the Fleet Earl Beatty, born David Beatty (1871–1936). Distinguished himself early commanding a small flotilla of stern-wheel river gunboats, accompanying in 1896 Kitchener's Sudan expedition. During the First World War the most successful British naval commander. At that time, First Sea Lord since 1919.

Speech at the Lifeboat Institution

I feel it a privilege to be called upon to speak in support of the resolution in honour of life-boat men of to-day, worthy inheritors of a hundred years' tradition of devoted service, and recording once more our gratitude to seamen's friends ashore who for more than three generations gave their time, their work, and their money to the welfare of this national organisation, so universally known and trusted, that a seaman of any nationality directly he has sighted our shores feels himself the object of its sleepless care.

The first words about our life-boat service I ever heard in my life (and that was before many of you in this hall were born) I mean living words, not words in print, were on the lips of a Breton seaman in the West Indies. He had been, it seems wrecked on our East coast at one time and what he said was—"On those (he meant our men) you can always depend. They don't give you up." A great testimony. I know now, of my own knowledge, that a lifeboat crew may fail sometimes, (there is no shame in being defeated by the sea) but that it never gives up.

I am especially gratified that in this particular life-saving service which is honoured to-day it is the Lowestoft men who have not failed. For it was on board of a Lowestoft coaster that I began my life under the merchant flag, the North Sea being my school, and Lowestoft and Pukefield[1] men, seven in all, being my masters for some three months, a full school term, one may say. I can never forget the friendliness of the Lowestoft people to a strange youngster. They may have been amused at me, but they taught me the very terms of sea speech. It is on this ground of old association that I venture to congratulate you personally, not so much on the public recognition you have received to-day from the hands of a great sea-officer in presence of this most distinguished company, as on the success of your efforts in saving the crew of that steamship, who looked to you for their lives with that absolute confidence which is the due and after all the greater reward of men who never give up.

Note to Speech at the Lifeboat Institution

1. There is no place of this name in Great Britain. Conrad meant Pakefield, a coastal townlet in Suffolk, two miles southwest of Lowestoft. Evidently, there was another handwritten version of the draft of the speech, from which Conrad's secretary typed. His "a" and "u" were often indistinguishable.

Conrad's fifteen-year friendship with Francis Warrington Dawson, Jr., is extensively described in Dale B. J. Randall's well-documented book *Joseph Conrad and Warrington Dawson: The Record of a Friendship,* Duke University Press, 1968.

F. W. Dawson—a South Carolinian and Catholic, son of a Civil War hero and well-known editor, himself an enterprising journalist and amateur novelist—was one of Conrad's very few American friends. He came to see Conrad at Aldington in Kent on 28 May 1910, being one of the first strangers Conrad invited after his long illness that year, and soon became a frequent visitor. Since 1914 he worked for many years at the American Embassy in Paris, although he became partly paralyzed in 1915 and was unable to walk after 1918.

Throughout almost his entire life (1878–1962) Dawson tried, unsuccessfully, to establish himself as a writer. Although Conrad refused to write an article about Dawson's work, he permitted his friend to publish a foreword to *Adventure in the Night*—a novel dedicated to "My Friend Joseph Conrad." The foreword, in the form of a letter, is actually a hybrid concoction from four different letters, dated 24 August 1911, 9 April 1912, undated 1922 and 2 June 1922.[1] None of these remarks was written about *Adventure in the Night,* but Dawson made them sound as if they were.

The "foreword" is reprinted here from W. Dawson, *Adventure in the Night,* London, 1924.

Note

1. Dale B. J. Randall, *Joseph Conrad . . .* , p. 108.

Warrington Dawson: *Adventure in the Night*
[untitled preface]

You can do anything you like, I believe. Your individuality will make you work. Remember that in the end value will tell—and you *are* giving value.

You have a most attractive style with something individual—and even racial—glowing through it and adding to the fascination of the perfectly simple diction. Of course, one is aware of the deep feeling under the quiet, correct I may say, poise of the phrase. And one cannot help feeling with you, all the way with you—even apart (in my case) from the complete accord of thought—from the conviction your perfectly unrhetorical prose carries to my mind.

It is all very characteristic, very "Dawsonian," and it is penetrated through and through by your characteristic earnestness of emotion. As to criticism of details, I would offer it with great diffidence if I were to offer it at all. For in those matters I am not, by any means, sure myself. This mainly for the reason that, having a pronounced temperament and a sort of personality in my writing which has not been acquired but was inborn (and therefore is very masterful), I know that I would be prejudiced in many ways by the mere fact of being what I am.

Joseph Conrad

[1911–22]

When Ford Madox Ford—at the time still calling himself Ford Madox Hueffer—first mentioned writing *The Nature of a Crime,* he described the story as "awful piffle."[1] It is indeed impossible to impute any artistic ambitions to this piece. Yet Ford insisted, probably to increase chances of financial success, on Conrad's co-operation. Four years had already passed since Conrad and Ford collaborated on *Romance,* but now and then, in moments of extreme stress, Ford would assist his older colleague, and Conrad, in turn, would give advice and serve as intermediary to publishers; he also aided Elsie in managing the family's shaky finances when Ford suffered a nervous breakdown.

The collaboration on *The Nature of a Crime,* begun in summer 1906, undoubtedly had the character of friendly assistance and not of serious literary coproduction. Conrad appears to have been antipathetic to the project and had to be cajoled to add anything to the text. Arthur Mizener, the author of *The Saddest Story,* an excellent book on Ford's life and work, believes that Conrad actually wrote only one short fragment—the same manuscript, presumably, which is preserved at Yale (it is the final section of chapter five, beginning with the words "Even to the dullest of men . . .").[2] When Ford wrote to Conrad on 8 November 1923 asking for his permission to reprint *The Nature of a Crime,* Conrad at first could not remember the piece at all. However, he eventually found a whole batch of manuscripts and typescripts relating to Edward Burden (one of the characters), some of these written in his own hand.[3] This confirms Ford's claim in a letter to J. B. Pinker—his and Conrad's literary agent—that they were planning to expand the story by inserting additional material between chapters five and six.[4] But it also indicates that possibly Conrad had more to do with the content of *The Nature of a Crime* than composing only one short passage.

The atmosphere of the piece, with its complete moral indifference and open egocentrism, is startlingly un-Conradian. For instance, the narrator-protagonist states his dominant wish in these words: "that somewhere in the world there should be something that I could give to you, or you to me, that would leave us free to do what we wish without the drag of the thought of what we owe, to each other, to the world!" There are a few Conrad-sounding sentences, like "the time is not of great deeds but of colossal speculations"—but on the whole the text is permeated with characteristically Fordian motifs: self-satisfaction, emotional blackmail, "spiritual superiority" of a poet to ordinary mortals, pseudo-metaphysical musings, etc. Professor Mizener notices similarities to *The Good Soldier*;[5] the husband of the narrator's beloved may foreshadow Rev. Dr. Duchemin in *Parade's End*.

The Nature of a Crime was the last piece on which Conrad and Ford collaborated. Contrary to Conrad's statement in the Preface, there is little irony in the story, and the original verdict of "piffle" should, I believe, be allowed to stand. But as a biographical and literary document, *The Nature of a Crime* is not without interest. It offers a striking testimony to Ford's inclinations on the one hand, and to Conrad's surprising capability of mimicry on the other. It reveals, too, what influences Conrad had to ward off during his ten years of close friendship with Ford.

Ford did not manage to sell *The Nature of a Crime* and it originally appeared in *The English Review*—edited by himself—in April and May 1909, under a grotesque pseudonym, Ignatz von Aschendorf. In 1924 it was reprinted in a separate volume, under the names of both authors. The present text follows that edition, which included prefaces by both Conrad and Ford (Conrad wrote his on May 1924[6]), and an Appendix in which Ford told his story of collaborating with Conrad on *Romance*.

Notes

1. Arthur Mizener, *The Saddest Story: A Biography of Ford Madox Ford,* New York–Cleveland, 1971, p. 116.
2. Conrad to Ford, 10 Nov. 1923, Ibid., p. 545.

3. Joseph Conrad, *Listy,* ed. Zdzisław Najder, Warszawa 1968, p. 459. The original letter at Yale.
4. Mizener, op. cit., pp. 118–19.
5. Ibid., p. 120.
6. Conrad to Ford, May 17th 1924, Yale.

Preface to *The Nature of a Crime*

For years my consciousness of this small piece of collaboration has been very vague, almost impalpable, like fleeting visits from a ghost. If I ever thought of it, and I must confess that I can hardly remember ever doing it on purpose till it was brought definitely to my notice by my Collaborator, I always regarded it as something in the nature of a fragment. I was surprised and even shocked to discover that it was rounded. But I need not have been. Rounded as it is in form, using the word form in its simplest sense—printed form—it remains yet a fragment from its very nature and also from necessity. It could never have become anything else. And even as a fragment it is but a fragment of something else that might have been—of a mere intention.

But, as it stands, what impresses me most is the amount this fragment contains of the crudely materialistic atmosphere of the time of its origin, the time when the *English Review* was founded. It emerges from the depths of a past as distant from us now as the square-skirted, long frock coats in which unscrupulous, cultivated, high-minded *jouisseurs* like ours here attended to their strange business activities and cultivated the little blue flower of sentiment. No doubt our man was conceived for purposes of irony; but our conception of him, I fear, is too fantastic.

Yet the most fantastic thing of all, it seems to me, is that we two who had so often discussed soberly the limits and methods of literary composition should be believed for a moment that a piece of work in the nature of an analytical confession (produced *in articulo mortis* as it were) could have been developed and achieved in collaboration!

What optimism! But it did not last long. I seem to remember a moment when I burst into earnest entreaties that all these people should be thrown overboard without more ado. This, I believe, *is*

the real nature of the crime. Overboard. The neatness and dispatch with which it is done in Chapter VIII was wholly the act of
my Collaborator's good nature in the face of my panic.

After signing these few prefatory words I will pass the pen to
him in the hope that he may be moved to contradict me on every
point of fact, impression, and appreciation. I said "the hope."
Yes, eager hope. For it would be delightful to catch the echo of
the desperate, earnest and funny quarrels which enlivened those
old days. The pity of it is that there comes a time when all the fun
of one's life must be looked for in the past.

                                                              J.C.
[1924]

The Nature of a Crime

You are, I suppose, by now in Rome. It is very curious how present to me are both Rome and yourself. There is a certain hill—
you, and that is the curious part of it, will never go there—yet,
yesterday, late in the evening, I stood upon its summit and you
came walking from a place below. It is always midday there: the
seven pillars of the Forum stand on high, their capitals linked together, and form one angle of a square. At their bases there lie
some detritus, a broken marble lion, and I think but I am not certain, the bronze she-wolf suckling the two bronze children. Your
dress brushed the herbs: it was grey and tenuous: I suppose you
do not know how you look when you are unconscious of being
looked at? But I looked at you for a long time—at my You.

I saw your husband yesterday at the club and he said that you
would not be returning till the end of April. When I got back to
my chambers I found a certain letter. I will tell you about it afterwards—but I forbid you to look at the end of what I am writing
now. There is a piece of news coming: I would break it to you if I
could—but there is no way of breaking the utterly unexpected.
Only, if you read this through you will gather from the tenor,
from the tone of my thoughts, a little inkling, a small preparation
for my disclosure. Yes: it is a "disclosure."

. . . Briefly, then, it was this letter—a business letter—that set me thinking: that made that hill rise before me. Yes, I stood upon it and there before me lay Rome—beneath a haze, in the immense sea of plains. I have often thought of going to Rome—of going with you, in a leisurely autumn of your life and mine. Now—since I have received that letter—I know that I shall never see any other Rome than that from an imagined hilltop. And when, in the wonderful light and shadelessness of that noon, last evening, you came from a grove of silver poplars, I looked at you—*my* you— for a very long while. You had, I think, a parasol behind your head, you moved slowly, you looked up at the capitals of those seven pillars . . . And I thought that I should never—since you will not return before the end of April—never see you again. I shall never see again the you that every other man sees . . .

You understand everything so well that already you must understand the nature of my disclosure. It is, of course, no disclosure to tell you that I love you. A very great reverence is due to youth —and a very great latitude is due to the dead. For I am dead: I have only lived through you for how many years now! And I shall never speak with you again. Some sort of burial will have been given to me before the end of April. I am a spirit. I have ended my relations with the world. I have balanced all my books, my will is made. Only I have nothing to leave—save to you, to whom I leave all that is now mine in the world—my memory.

It is very curious—the world now. I walked slowly down here from Gordon Square. I walked slowly—for all my work is done. On the way I met Graydon Bankes, the K.C. It would have astonished him if he could have known how unreal he looked to me. He is six feet high, and upon his left cheek there is a brown mole. I found it difficult to imagine why he existed. And all sorts of mists hurried past him. It was just outside the Natural History Museum. He said that his Seaford Railway Bill would come before Committee in June. And I wondered: what is June? . . . I laughed and thought: why, June will never come!

June will never come. Imagine that for a moment. We have discussed the ethics of suicide. You see why June will never come!

You remember that ring I always wear? The one with a bulging, greenish stone. Once or twice you have asked me what stone it was. You thought, I know, that it was in bad taste and I told you I wore it for the sake of associations. I know you thought—but no: there has never been any woman but you.

You must have felt a long time ago that there was not, that there could not have been another woman. The associations of the ring are not with the past of a finished affection, or hate, or passion, with all these forms of unrest that have a term in life: they looked forward to where there is no end—whether there is rest in it God alone knows. If it were not bad taste to use big words in extremities I would say there was Eternity in the ring—Eternity which is the negation of all that life may contain of losses and disappointments. Perhaps you have noticed that there was one note in our confidence that never responded to your touch. It was that note of universal negation contained within the glass film of the ring. It is not you who brought the ring into my life: I had it made years ago. It was in my nature always to anticipate a touch on my shoulder, to which the only answer could be an act of defiance. And the ring is my weapon. I shall raise it to my teeth, bite through the glass: inside there is poison.

I haven't concealed anything from you. Have I? And, with the great wisdom for which I love you, you have tolerated these other things. You would have tolerated this too, you who have met so many sinners and have never sinned . . .

Ah, my dear one—that is why I have so loved you. From our two poles we have met upon one common ground of scepticism— so that I am not certain whether it was you or I who first said: "Believe nothing: be harsh to no one." But at least we have suffered. One does not drag around with one such a cannonball as I have done all these years without thinking some wise thoughts. And well I know that in your dreary and terrible life you have gained your great wisdom. You have been envied; you too have thought: Is any prospect fair to those among its trees? And I have been envied for my gifts, for my talents, for my wealth, for my official position, for the letters after my name, for my great and empty house, for my taste in pictures—for my . . . for my opportunities.

Great criminals and the very patient learn one common lesson: Believe in nothing, be harsh to no one!

But you cannot understand how immensely leisurely I feel. It is one o'clock at night. I cannot possibly be arrested before eleven tomorrow morning. I have ten hours in which, without the shadow of a doubt, I can write to you: I can put down my thoughts desultorily and lazily. I have half a score of hours in which to speak to you.

The stress of every secret emotion makes for sincerity in the end. Silence is like a dam. When the flood is at its highest the dam gives way. I am not conceited enough to think that I can sweep you along, terrified, in the rush of my confidences. I have not the elemental force. Perhaps it is just that form of "greatness" that I have lacked all my life—that profound quality which the Italians call *terribilità*. There is nothing overpowering or terrible in the confession of a love too great to be kept within the bounds of the banality which is the safeguard of our daily life. Men have been nerved to crime for the sake of a love that was theirs. The call of every great passion is to unlawfulness. But your love was not mine, and my love for you was vitiated by that conventional reverence which, as to nine parts in ten, is genuine, but as to the last tenth a solemn sham behind which hide all the timidities of a humanity no longer in its youth. I have been of my time—altogether of my time—lacking courage for a swoop, as a bird respects a ragged and nerveless scarecrow. Altogether a man of my time. Observe, I do not say "our time." You are of all time—you are the loved Woman of the first cry that broke the silence and of the last song that shall mark the end of this ingenious world to which love and suffering have been given, but which has in the course of ages invented for itself all the virtues and all the crimes. And being of this world and of my time I have set myself to deal ingeniously with my suffering and my love.

Now everything is over—even regrets. Nothing remains of finite things but a few days of life and my confession to make to you—to you alone of all the world.

It is difficult. How am I to begin? Would you believe it—every time I left your presence it was with the desire, with the necessity to forget you. Would you believe it?

This is the great secret—the heart of my confession. The distance did not count. No walls could make me safe. No solitude could defend me; and having no faith in the consolations of eternity I suffered too cruelly from your absence.

If there had been kingdoms to conquer, a crusade to preach—but no. I should not have had to courage to go beyond the sound of your voice. You might have called to me anytime! You never did. Never. And now it is too late. Moreover, I am a man of my time, the time is not of great deeds but of colossal speculations. The moments when I was not with you had to be got through somehow. I dared not face them empty-handed lest from sheer distress I should go mad and begin to execrate you. Action? What form of action could remove me far enough from you whose every thought was referred to your existence? And as you were to me a soul of truth and serenity, I tried to forget you in lies and excitement. My only refuge from the tyranny of my desire was in abasement. Perhaps I was mad. I gambled. I gambled first with my own money and then with money that was not mine. You know my connection with the great Burden fortune. I was trustee under my friend's, Alexander Burden's, will. I gambled with a determined recklessness, with closed eyes. You understand how the origin of my houses, of my collections, of my reputation, of my taste for magnificence—which you deigned sometimes to mock indulgently with an exquisite flattery as at something not quite worthy of me. It was like a breakneck ride on a wild horse, and now the fall has come. It was sudden. I am alive but my back is broken. Edward Burden is going to be married. I must pay back what I have borrowed from the Trust. I cannot. Therefore I am dead. (A mouse has just come out from beneath one of the deed-boxes. It looks up at me. It may have been eating some of the papers in the large cupboard. Tomorrow morning I shall tell Saunders to get a cat. I have never seen a mouse here before. I have never been here so late before. At times of pressure, as you know, I have always taken my papers home. So that these late hours have been, as it were, the prerogative of the mouse. No. I shall not get a cat. To that extent I am still a part of the world: I am master of the fate of mice!) I have, then, ten hours, less the time it has taken me to chronicle the mouse, in which to talk to you. It is strange, when I look back on it, that in all the years we have known each other—seven years, three months and two days —I have never had so long as ten hours in which I might talk to you. The longest time was when we came back from Paris together, when your husband was in such a state that he could neither see nor hear. (I've seen him, by-the-bye, every day since you have been gone. He's really keeping away from it wonderfully well; in fact, I should say that he has not once actually succumbed. I fancy, really, that your absence is good for him in a way: it creates a new set of circumstances, and a change is said to be an excellent air in the breaking of a habit. He has, I mean, to occupy himself with some of the things, innumerable as they are, that you do for him. I find that he has even had his passbook from the bank and has compared it with his counterfoils. I haven't, on account of this improvement, yet been round to his chemist's. But I shall certainly tell them that they *must* surreptitiously decrease the strength of it.) That was the longest time we have ever really talked together. And, when I think that in all these years I haven't once so much as held your hand for a moment longer that the strictest of etiquette demanded! And I loved you within the first month.

I wonder why that is. Fancy, perhaps. Habit, perhaps—a kind of idealism, a kind of delicacy, a fastidiousness. As you know very well it is not on account of any moral scruples . . .

I break off to look through what I have already written to you. There is, first, the question of why I never told you my secret: then, the question of what my secret really is; I have started so many questions and have not followed one of them out to the very end. But all questions resolve themselves into the one question of our dear and inestimable relationship.

I think it has been one of the great charms of our relationship that all our talks have been just talks. We have discussed everything under the sun, but we have never discussed anything *au fond*. We have strayed into all sorts of byways and have never got anywhere. I try to remember how many evenings in the last five years we have not spent together. I think they must be less than a hundred in number. You know how, occasionally, your husband would wake out of his stupors—or walk *in* his stupor and deliver one of his astonishingly brilliant disquisitions. But remember how, always, whether he talked of free love or the improvement in the breed of carriage-horses, he always thrashed his subject out to the bitter end. It was not living with a man: it was assisting at a performance. And, when he was sunk into his drugs or when he was merely literary, or when he was away, how lazily we talked. I think no two minds were ever so fitted one into another as yours and mine. It is not of course that we agree on all subjects—or perhaps upon any. In the whole matter of conduct we are so absolutely different—you are always for circumspection, for a careful preparation of the ground, for patience; and I am always ready to act, and afterwards draw the moral from my own actions. But somehow, in the end, it has all worked out in our being in perfect agreement. Later I will tell you why that is.

Let me return to my mouse. For you will observe that the whole question revolves, really, around that little allegorical mite. It is an omen: it is a symbol. It is a little herald of the Providence that I do not believe in—of the Providence you so implicitly seek to obey. For instinctively you believe in providence—in God, if you will. I as instinctively disbelieve. Intellectually of course you disbelieve in a God. You say that it is impossible for Reason to accept an Overlord; I that Reason forces one to accept an Overlord; that Reason forces one to believe in an Omnipotent Ruler—only I am unable to believe. We, my dear, are in ourselves evidence of a design in creation. For we are the last word of creation. It has taken all the efforts, all the birth pangs of all the ages to evolve— you and me. And, being evolved, we are intellectually so perfectly and so divinely fashioned to dovetail together. And, physically too, are we not divinely meant the one for the other? Do we not react to the same causes: should not we survive the same hardships or succumb to the same stresses? Since you have been away I have gone looking for people—men, women, children, even animals—that could hold my attention for a minute. There has not been one. And what purer evidence of design could you ask for than that?

I have made this pact with the Providence that I argue for, with the Providence in whose existence I cannot believe—that if, from under the castle of black metal boxes, the mouse reappear and challenge death—then there is no future state. And, since I can find no expression save in you, if we are not reunited I shall no longer exist. So my mouse is the sign, the arbitrament, a symbol of an eternal life or the herald of nothingness.

I will make to you the confession that since this fancy, this profound truth, has entered my mind, I have not raised my eyes from the paper. I dread—I suppose it is dread—to look across the ring of light that my lamp casts. But now I will do so. I will let my eyes travel across the bundles of dusty papers on my desk. Do you know I have left them just as they were on the day when you came to ask me to take your railway tickets? I will let my eyes travel across that rampart of blue and white dockets. . . . The mouse is not there.

But that is not an end of it. I am not a man to be ungenerous in my dealings with the Omnipotent: I snatch no verdict.

II

Last night it was very late and I grew tired, so I broke off my letter. Perhaps I was really afraid of seeing that mouse again. Those minute superstitions are curious things. I noticed, when I looked at the enumeration of these pages tonight, I began to write upon the thirteenth sheet—and that gives me a vague dissatisfaction. I read, by-the-bye, a paragraph in a newspaper: it dealt with half-mad authors. One of these, the writer said, was Zola; he was stated to be half mad because he added together the numbers on the backs of cabs passing him in the street. Personally, I do that again and again—and I know very well that I do it in order to dull my mind. It is a sort of narcotic. Johnson, we know, touched his street-posts in a certain order: that, too, was to escape from miserable thoughts. And we all know how, as children, we have obeyed mysterious promptings to step upon the lines between the paving-stones in the street. . . . But the children have their futures: it is well that they should propitate the mysterious Omnipotent One. In their day, too, Johnson and Zola had their futures. It was well that Johnson should "touch" against the evil chance; that Zola should rest his mind against new problems. In me it is mere imbecility. For I have no future.

Do you find it difficult to believe that? You know the Burdens, of course. But I think you do not know that, for the last nine years, I have administered the Burden estates all by myself. The original trustees were old Lady Burden and I; but nine years ago Lady Burden gave me a power of attorney and since then I have acted alone. It was just before then that I had bought the houses in Gordon Square—the one I live in, the one you live in, and the seven others. Well, rightly speaking, those houses have been bought with Burden money, and all my pictures, all my prints, all my books, my furniture, my reputation as a connoisseur, my governorship of the two charities—all the me that people envy—have been bought with the Burden money. I assure you that at times I have found it a pleasurable excitement . . . You see, I have wanted you sometimes so terribly—so terribly that the juggling with the Burden accounts has been as engrossing a narcotic as to Zola was the adding up of the numbers upon the backs of cabs. Mere ordinary work would never have held my thoughts.

Under old Burden's will young Edward Burden comes of age when he reaches the age of twenty-five or when he marries with my consent. Well, he will reach the age of twenty-five and he will marry on April 5. On that day the solicitors of his future wife will make their scrutiny of my accounts. It is regarded, you understand, as a mere formality. But it amuses me to think of the faces of Coke and Coke when they come to certain figures! It was an outlaw of some sort, was it not, who danced and sang beneath the gallows? I wonder, now, what sort of traitor, outlaw, or stealthy politician I should have made in the Middle Ages. It is certain that, save for this one particular of property, I should be in very truth illustrious. No doubt the state shall come at last in which there shall no more be any property. I was born before my time.

For it is certain that I am illustrious save in that one respect. Today young Edward Burden came here to the office to introduce me to his fiancée. You observe that I have robbed her. The Burden property is really crippled. They came, this bright young couple, to get a cheque from me with which to purchase a motorcar. They are to try several cars in the next three weeks. On the day before the wedding they are to choose one that will suit them best —and on the wedding day in the evening they are to start for Italy. They will be coming towards you. . . . Then no doubt, too, a telegram will reach them, to say that in all probability motorcars will be things not for them for several years to come. What a crumbling of their lives!

It was odd how I felt towards *her*. You know his pompous, high forehead, the shine all over him, the grave, weighty manner. He held his hat—a wonderful shiny, "good" hat—before his mouth, for all the world as if he had been in church. He made, even, a speech in introducing Miss Averies to me. You see, in a sense, he was in a temple. My office enshrined a deity, a divinity: the law, property, the rights of man as maintained by an august consti- tution. I am for him such a wonderfully "safe" man. My dear one, you cannot imagine how I feel towards him: a little like a deity, a little like an avenging Providence. I imagine that the real Deity must feel towards some of His worshippers much as I feel towards this phoenix of the divines.

The Deity is after all the supreme Artist—and the supreme quality of Art is surprise.

Imagine then the feeling of the Deity towards some of those who most confidently enter His temple. Just imagine His attitude towards those who deal in the obvious platitudes that "honesty is the best policy," or "genius the capacity for taking pains." So for days the world appears to them. Then suddenly: honesty no longer pays; the creature, amassing with his infinite pains data for his Great Work, is discovered to have produced a work of an Infinite Dullness. That is the all-suffering Deity manifesting Him- self to His worshippers. For assuredly a day comes when two added to two no longer results in four. That day will come on April 5 for Edward Burden.

After all he has done nothing to make two and two become four. He has not even checked his accounts: well, for some years now I have been doing as much as that. But with his fiancée it is different. She is a fair, slight girl with eyes that dilate under all sorts of emotion. In my office she appears not a confident worshipper but a rather frightened fawn led before an Anthropo- morphic Deity. And, strangely enough, though young Burden who trusts me inspires me with a sardonic dislike, I felt myself saying to this poor little thing that faced me: "Why: I have wronged you!" And I regretted it.

She, you see, has after all given something towards a right to enjoy Burden estates and the Burden wealth; she has given her fragile beauty, her amiability, her worship, no doubt, of the intol- erable Edward. And all this payment in the proper coin: so she has in a sense a right. . . .

Goodnight dear one, I think you have it in your power—you *might* have it in your power—to atone to this little creature. To- morrow I will tell you why and how.

III

I wrote last night that you have something in your power. If you wished it you could make me live on. I am confident that you will not wish it: for you will understand that capriciously or intolerably I am tired of living this life. I desire you so terribly that now even the excitement of fooling Burden no longer hypnotizes me into an acceptance of life without you. Frankly, I am tired out. If I had to go on living any longer I should have to ask you to be mine in one form or other. With that and with my ability—for of course I have great ability—I could go on fooling Burden for ever. I could restore: I could make sounder than ever it was that preposterous "going concern" the Burden Estate. Unless I like to let them, I think that the wife's solicitors will not discover what I have done. For, frankly, I have put myself out in this matter in order to be amusing to myself and ingenious. I have forged whole builder's estimates for repairs that were never executed: I have invented whole hosts of defaulting tenants. It has not been latterly for money that I have done this: it has been simply for the sheer amusement of looking at Edward Burden and saying to myself:

"Ah: you trust me, my sleek friend. Well . . ."

But indeed I fancy that I am rich enough to be able to restore to them all that I have taken. And, looking at Edward Burden's little fiancée, I was almost tempted to set upon that weary course of juggling. But I am at the end of my tether. I cannot live without you longer. And I do not wish to ask you. Later I will tell you. Or no—I will tell you now.

You see, my dear thing, it is a question of going one better. It would be easy enough to deceive your husband: it would be easier still to go away together. I think that neither you nor I have ever had any conscientious scruples. But, analysing the matter down to its very depths, I think we arrive at this, that without the motives for self-restraint that other people have, we are anxious to show more self-restraint than they. We are doing certain work not for payment but for sheer love of work. Do I make myself clear? For myself I have a great pride in your image. I can say to myself: "Here is a woman, my complement. She has no respect for the law. She does not value what a respect for the law would bring

her. Yet she remains purer than the purest of the makers of law."
And I think it is the converse of that feeling that you have for me.

If you desire me to live on, I will live on: I am so swayed by
you that if you desire me to break away from this ideal of you, the
breath of a command will send me round to your side.

I am ready to give my life for this Ideal: nay more, I am ready
to sacrifice you to it, since I know that life for you will remain a
very bitter thing. I know, a little, what renunciation means.

And I am asking you to bear it—for the sake of my ideal of
you. For, assuredly, unless I can have you I must die—and I
know that you will not ask me to have you. And I love you: and
bless you for it.

IV

I have just come in from *Tristan and Isolde*.

I had to hurry and be there for the first notes because you—my
you—would, I felt, be sitting beside me as you have so often.
That, of course, is passion—the passion that makes us unaccount-
able in our actions.

I found you naturally: but I found, too, something else. It has
always a little puzzled me why we return to *Tristan*. There are
passages in that thing as intolerable as anything in any of the Ger-
manic master's scores. But we are held—simply by the idea of the
love-philtre: it's that alone that interests us. We do not care about
the initial amenities of Tristan and the prima donna: we do not
believe in Mark's psychologising: but, from the moment when
those two dismal marionettes have drained unconsideringly the
impossible cup, they become suddenly alive, and we see two
human beings under the grip of a passion—acting as irrationally
as I did when I promised my cabman five shillings to get me to the
theatre in time for the opening bars.

It is, you see, the love-philtre that performs this miracle. It interests—it is real to us—because every human being knows what
it is to act, irrationally, under the stress of some passion or other.
We are drawn along irresistibly: we commit the predestined follies
or the predestined heroisms: the other side of our being acts in
contravention of all our rules of conduct or of intellect. Here, in
Tristan, we see such madness justified with a concrete substance, a

herb, a root. We see a vision of a state of mind in which morality no longer exists: we are given a respite, a rest: an interval in which no standard of conduct oppresses us. It is an idea of an appeal more universal than any other in which the tired imagination of humanity takes refuge.

The thought that somewhere in the world there should be something that I could give to you, or you to me, that would leave us free to do what we wish without the drag of the thought of what we owe, to each other, to the world! And after all, what greater gift could one give to another? It would be the essential freedom. For assuredly, the philtre could do no more that put it in a man's power to do what he would do if he were let loose. He would not bring out more than he had in him: but he would fully and finally express himself.

Something unexpected has changed the current of my thoughts. Nothing can change their complexion, which is governed not by what others do but by the action which I must face presently. And I don't know why I should use the word unexpected, unless because at the moment I was very far from expecting that sort of perplexity. The correct thing to say would be that something natural has happened.

Perfectly natural. Asceticism is the last thing that one could expect from the Burdens. Alexander Burden, the father, was an exuberant millionaire, in no vulgar way, of course; he was exuberant with restraint, not for show, with a magnificence which was for private satisfaction mainly. I am talking here of the ascetic temperament which is based on renunciation, not of mere simplicity of tastes, which is simply scorn for certain orders of sensations. There have been millionaires who have lived simply. There have been millionaires who have lived sordidly—but miserliness is one of the supreme forms of sensualism.

Poor Burden had a magnificent physique. The reserved abilities of generations of impoverished Burdens, starved for want of opportunities, matured in his immense success—and all their starved appetites too. But all the reserve quality of obscure Burdens has been exhausted in him. There was nothing to come to his son— who at most could have been a great match and is today looked upon in that light, I suppose, by the relations of his future wife. I don't know in what light that young man looks upon himself. His time of trial is coming.

Yesterday at eight in the evening he came to see me. I thought at first he wanted some money urgently. But very soon I reflected that he need not have looked so embarrassed in that case. And presently I discovered that it was not money that he was in need of. He looked as though he had come, with that characteristic gravity of his—so unlike his father—to seek absolution at my hands. But that intention he judged more decorous, I suppose, to present to me as a case of conscience.

Of course it was the case of a girl—not his fiancée. At first I thought he was in an ugly scrape. Nothing of the kind. The excellent creature who had accepted his protection for some two years past—how dull they must have seemed to her—was perhaps for that reason perfectly resigned to forego that advantage. At the same time, she was not too proud to accept a certain provision, compensation—whatever you like to call it. I had never heard of anything so proper in my life. He need not have explained the matter to me at all. But evidently he had made up his mind to indulge in the luxury of a conscience.

To indulge that sort of conscience leads one almost as far as indulged passion, only, I cannot help thinking, on a more sordid road. A luxury snatched from the fire is in a way purified, but to find this one he had gone apparently to the bottom of his heart. I don't charge him with a particularly odious degree of corruption, but I perceived clearly that what he wanted really was to project the sinful effect of that irregular connection—let us call it—into his regulated, reformed, I may say lawfully blessed state—for the sake of retrospective enjoyment, I suppose. This rather subtle, if unholy, appetite, he was pleased to call the voice of his conscience. I listened to his dialectic exercises till the great word that was sure to come out sooner or later was pronounced.

"It seems," he said, with every appearance of distress, "that from a strictly moral point of view I ought to make a clean breast of it to Annie."

I listened to him—and, by Heaven, listening to him I *do* feel like the Godhead of whom I have already written to you. You know, positively he said that at the very moment of his "fall" he had thought of what *I* should think of him. And I said:

"My good Edward, you are the most debauched person I have ever met."

His face fell, his soft lips dropped right down into a horseshoe. He had come to me as one of those bland optimists *would* go to his deity. He expected to be able to say: "I have sinned," and to be able to hear the Deity say: "That's all right, your very frank confession does you infinite credit." His deity was, in fact, to find him some way out of his moral hole. I was to find him some genial excuse; to make him feel good in his excellent digestion once more. That was, absolutely, his point of view, for at my brutal pronouncement he stuttered:

"But—but surely . . . the faults of youth . . . and surely there are plenty of others? . . ."

I shook my head at him and panic was dropping out of his eyes: "Can't I marry Annie honourably?" he quavered. I took a sinister delight in turning the knife inside him. I was going to let him go anyhow: the sort of cat that I am always lets its mice go. (That mouse, by-the-bye, has never again put in an appearance.)

"My dear fellow," I said, "does not your delicacy let you see the hole you put me into? It's to my interest that you should not marry Miss Averies and you ask me to advise you on the point."

His mouth dropped open: positively he had never considered that when he married I lost the confounded three hundred a year for administering the Burden Trust. I sat and smiled at him to give him plenty of time to let his mind agonize over his position.

"Oh, hang it," he said. . . . And his silly eyes rolled round my room looking for that Providence that he felt ought to intervene in his behalf. When they rested on me again I said:

"There, go away. Of course it's a fault of your youth. Of course every man that's fit to call himself a man has seduced a clergy-man's daughter."

He said:

"Oh, but there was not anything common about it."

"No," I answered, "you had an uncommonly good time of it with your moral scruples. I envy you the capacity. You'll have a duller one with Miss Averies, you know."

That was too much for him to take in, so he smoothed his hat.

"When you said I was . . . debauched . . . you were only

laughing at me. That was hardly fair. I'm tremendously in earnest."

"You're only play-acting compared with me," I answered. He had the air of buttoning his coat after putting a cheque into his breast pocket. He had got, you see, the cheque he expected: my applause of his successful seduction, my envy of his good fortune. That was what he had come for—and he got it. He went away with it pretty barefacedly, but he stopped at the threshold to let drop:

"Of course if I had known you would be offended by my having recourse to Annie's solicitors for the settlement . . ."

I told him I was laughing at him about that too.

"It was the correct thing to do, you know," were the words he shut the door upon. The ass . . .

The phrase of his—that he had thought of me at the moment of his fall—gives you at once the measure of his respect for me. But it gave me much more. It gave me my cue: it put it into my head to say he was debauched. And, indeed, that is debauchery. For it is the introduction of one's morals into the management of one's appetites that makes an indulgence of them debauchery. Had my friend Edward regarded his seduction as the thing he so much desired me to tell him it was; a thing of youth, high spirits—a thing we all do—had he so regarded it, I could not really have called it debauchery. But—and this is the profound truth—the measure of debauchery is the amount of excitement: if it brings into play not only all our physical but all our moral nature, then we have the crucial point beyond which no man can go. It isn't, in fact, the professional seducer, the artist in seduction that gets pleasure from the pursuit of his avocation, any more than it is the professional musician who gets thrills from the performance of music. You cannot figure to yourself the violinist, as he fiddles the most complicated passage of a concerto, when he really surmounts the difficulty by dint of using all his knowledge and all his skill—you cannot imagine him thinking of his adviser, his mother, his God and all the other things that my young friend says he thought about. And it is the same with the professional seducer. He may do all that he knows to bring his object about—but that is not debauchery. It is, by comparison, a joyless occupation: it is drinking when you are thirsty. Putting it in terms of the most threadbare allegory—you cannot imagine that Adam got out of the fall the pleasure that Edward Burden got out of his bite of the apple.

But Edward Burden, whilst he shilly-shallied with "Shall I?" and "Sha'n't I?" could deliciously introduce into the matter *all* his human relationships. He could think of me, of his mother, of the fact that potentially he was casting to the winds the very cause for his existence. For assuredly, if Edward Burden have a cause for existence it is that he should not, morally or physically, do anything that would unfit him to make a good marriage. So he had, along with what physical pleasure there might be, the immense excitement of staking his all along with the tremendous elation of the debate within himself that went before. For he was actually staking his all upon the chance that he could both take what he desired and afterwards reconcile it with his conscience to make a good match. Well, he has staked and won. That is the true debauchery. That, in a sense, is the compensating joy that Puritanism gets.

v

I have just come in. Again you will not guess from where. From choosing a motorcar with Burden and his fiancée. It seems incredible that I should be called upon to preside at these preparations for my own execution. I looked at hundreds of these shiny engines, with the monstrously inflated white wheels, and gave a half-amused—but I can assure you a half-interested—attention to my own case. For one of these will one day—and soon now—be arrested in a long rush, by my extinction. In it there will be seated the two young people who went with me through the garages. They will sit in some sort of cushioned ease—the cushions will be green—because Miss Averies let slip to me, in a little flutter of shy confidence, the words: "Oh, don't let's have green, because it's an unlucky colour." Edward Burden, of course, suppressed her with a hurried whisper as if, in thus giving herself away to me, she must be committing a sin against the house of Burden.

That, naturally, is the Burden tradition: a Burden's wife must possess frailties: but she must feign perfection even to a trusted adviser of the family. She must not confess the superstitions. It was amusing, the small incident, because it was the very first attempt that little Miss Averies has ever made to get near me. God knows what Edward may have made me appear to her: but I fancy that, whatever Edward may have said, she had pierced through that particular veil: she realizes, with her intuition, that I am dangerous. She is alarmed and possibly fascinated because she feels that I am not "straight"—that I might, in fact, be a woman or a poet. Burden, of course, has never got beyond seeing that I dress better than he does and choose a dinner better than his uncle Darlington.

I came, of course, out of the motorcar ordeal with flying colours —on these lines. I lived, in fact, up to my character for being orthodox in the matter of comfort. I even suggested two little mirrors, like those which were so comforting to us all when we sat in hansom cabs. That struck Burden as being the height of ingenuity —and I know it proved to Miss Averies, most finally, that I am dangerous, since no woman ever looks in those little mirrors without some small motive of coquetry. It was just after that that she said to me:

"Don't you think that the little measures on the tops of the new canisters are extravagant for China tea?"

That, of course, admitted me to the peculiar intimacy that women allow to other women, or to poets, or to dangerous men. Edward, I know, dislikes the drinking of China tea because it is against the principle of supporting the British flag. But Miss Averies in her unequal battle with this youth of the classical features slightly vulgarized, called me in to show a sign of sympathy —to give at least the flicker of the other side—of the woman, the poet, or the pessimist among men. She asked me, in fact, not to take up the cudgels to the extent of saying that China tea is the thing to drink—that would have been treason to Edward—but she desired that her instinct should be acknowledged to the extent of saying that the measures of canisters should be contrived to suit the one kind of tea as well as the other. In his blind sort of way Edward caught the challenge in the remark and his straight brown lowered a very little.

"If you don't have more than three pounds of China tea in the house in a year it won't matter about the measures," he said. "We never use more at Shackleton."

"But it makes the tea too strong, Edward."

"Then you need not fill the measure," he answered.

"Oh, I wish," she said to me, "that you'd tell Edward not to make me make tea at all. I dread it. The servants do it so much better."

"So," I asked, "Edward has arranged everything down to the last detail?"

Edward looked to me for approval and applause.

"You see, Annie has had so little experience, and I've had to look after my mother's house for years." His air said: "Yes! You'll see our establishment will be run on the very best lines! Don't you admire the way I'm taming her already?"

I gave him, of course, a significant glance. Heaven knows why: for it is absolutely true that I am tired of appearing reliable—to Edward Burden or any one else in the world. What I want to do is simply to say to Edward Burden: "No, I don't at all admire your dragging down a little bundle of ideals and sentiments to your own fatted calf's level."

I suppose I have in me something of the poet. I can imagine that if I had to love or to marry this little Averies girl I should try to find out what was her tiny vanity and I should minister to it. In some way I should discover from her that she considered herself charming, or discreet, or tasteful, or frivolous, beyond all her fellows. And, having discovered it, I should bend all my energies to giving her opportunities for displaying her charm, her discreetness or her coquetry. With a woman of larger and finer mould—with you!—I should no doubt bring into play my own idealism. I should invest her with the attributes that I consider the most desirable in the world. But in either case I cannot figure myself dragging her down to my own social or material necessities.

That is what Edward Burden is doing for little Miss Averies. I don't mean to say that he does not idealize her—but he sees her transfigured as the dispenser of his special brand of tea or the mother of the sort of child that he was. And that seems to me a very valid reason why women, if they were wise, should trust their fortunes coldbloodedly and of set reason to the class of dangerous men that now allure them and that they flee from.

They flee from them, I am convinced, because they fear for their worldly material fortunes. They fear, that is to say, that the poet is not a stable man of business: they recognise that he is a gambler—and it seems to them that it is folly to trust to a gambler for lifelong protection. In that they are perhaps right. But I think that no woman doubts her power to retain a man's affection—so that it is not to the reputation for matrimonial instability that the poet owes his disfavour. A woman lives, in short, to play with this particular fire, since to herself she says: "Here is a man who has broken the hearts of many women. I will essay the adventure of taming him." And, if she considers the adventure a dangerous one, that renders the contest only the more alluring, since at heart every woman, like every poet, is a gambler. In that perhaps she is right.

But it seems to me that women make a great mistake in the value of the stakes that are ready to pay in order to enter this game. They will stake, that is to say, their relatively great coin— their sentimental lives; but they hoard with closed fingers the threepenny bit which is merely the material future.

They prefer, that is to say, to be rendered the mere presiding geniuses of well-loaded boards. It is better to be a lady—which you will remember philologically means a "loaf-cutter"—than to be an Ideal.

And in this they are obviously wrong. If a woman can achieve the obvious miracle of making a dangerous man stable in his affections she may well be confident that she can persuade him to turn his serious attention to the task of keeping a roof over her head. Certainly, I know, if I were a woman which of the two types of men I would choose. Upon the lowest basis it is better for all purposes of human contracts to be married to a good liar than to a bad one. For a lie is a figurative truth—and it is the poet who is the master of these illusions. Even in the matter of marital relations it is probable that the poet is as faithful as the Edward Burdens of this world—only the Edward Burdens are more skilful at concealing from the rest of the world their pleasant vices. I doubt whether they are as skilful at concealing them from the woman concerned—from the woman, with her intuition, her power to seize fine shades of coolness and her awakened self-interest. Imagine the wife of Edward Burden saying to him, "You have deceived me!" Imagine then the excellent youth, crimsoning, stuttering. He has been taught all his life that truth must prevail though the skies fall—and he stammers: "Yes: I have betrayed you." And that is

tragedy, though in the psychological sense—and that is the important one—Edward Burden may have been as faithful as the
ravens, who live for fifteen decades with the same mate. He will,
in short, blunder into a tragic, false position. And he will make
the tragedy only the more tragic in that all the intellectual powers
he may possess will be in the direction of perpetuating the dismal
position. He will not be able to argue that he has not been un-
faithful—but he will be able to find a hundred arguments for the
miserable woman prolonging her life with him. Position, money,
the interests of the children, the feelings of her family and of his—
all these considerations will make him eloquent to urge her to prolong her misery. And probably she will prolong it.

This, of course, is due to the excellent Edward's lack of an in-
stinctive sympathy. The poet, with a truer vision, will in the same
case be able to face his Miss Averies' saying: "You have deceived
me!" with a different assurance. Supposing the deflection to have
been of the momentary kind he will be able to deny with a good
conscience since he will be aware of himself and his feelings. He
will at least be able to put the case in its just light. Or, if the
deflection be really temperamental, really permanent, he will be
unable—it being his business to look at the deeper verities—to lie
himself out of the matter. He will break, strictly and sharply. Or,
if he do not, it may be taken as a sign that his Miss Averies is still
of value to him—that she, in fact, is still the woman that it is his
desire to have for his companion. This is true of course, only in
the large sense, since obviously there are poets whose reverence
for position, the interest of children or the feelings of their friends
and relatives, may outweigh their hatred of a false position. These,
however, are poets in the sense that they write verse: I am speaking of those who live the poet's life; to such, a false position is too
intolerable to be long maintained.

But this again is only one of innumerable side issues: let me return to my main contention that a dinner of herbs with a dangerous man is better than having to consume the flesh of stalled oxen
with Edward Burden. Perhaps that is only a way of saying that
you would have done better to entrust yourself to me than to—
(But no, your husband is a better man than Edward Burden. He
has at least had the courage to revert to his passion. I went this afternoon to your chemists and formally notified them that if they

supplied him with more than the exactly prescribed quantity of that stuff, I, as holding your power of attorney, should do all that the law allows me to do against them.)

Even to the dullest of men, marrying is for the most part an imaginative act. I mean marrying as a step in life sanctioned by law, custom and that general consent of mankind which is the hallmark of every irrational institution. By irrational I do not mean wrong or stupid. Marriage is august by the magnitude of the issues it involves, balancing peace and strife on the fine point of a natural impulse refined by the need of a tangible ideal. I am not speaking here of mere domestic peace or strife which for most people that count are a question of manners and a mode of life. And I am thinking of the peace mostly—the peace of the soul which yearns for some sort of certitude in this earth, the peace of the heart which yearns for conquest, the peace of the imaginative faculty which in its restless quest of a high place of rest is spurred on by these great desires and that great fear.

And even Edward Burden's imagination is moved by these very desires and that very fear—or else he would not have dreamt of marrying. I repeat, marriage is an imaginative institution. It's true that his imagination is a poor thing, but it is genuine nevertheless. The faculty of which I speak is of one kind in all of us. Not to every one is given that depth of feeling, that faculty of absolute trust which *will not* be deceived, and the exulting masterfulness of the senses which are the mark of a fearless lover. Fearless lovers are rare, if obstinate, and sensual fools are countless as grains of sand by the seashore. I can imagine that correct young man perfectly capable of setting himself deliberately to worry a distracted girl into surrender.

VI

I don't know why, tonight in particular, the fact that I am a dead man occurs to me very insistently. I had forgotten this for two whole days. If anyone very dear to you has ever been *in extremis* at a distance and you have journeyed to be at the last bedside, you will know how possible this is—how for hours at a time the mind will go wandering away from the main fact that is drawing you onwards, till suddenly it comes back: someone is dying at

a distance. And I suppose one's I is the nearest friend that one has
—and my I is dying at a distance. At the end of a certain number
of days is the deathbed towards which I am hurrying—it is a fact
which I cannot grasp. But one aspect grows more clear to me
every time I return to the subject.

You remember that, when we have discussed suicide, we have
agreed that to the man of action death is a solution: to the man of
thoughts it is none. For the man of action expresses himself in action, and death is the negation of action: the man of thought sees
the world only in thoughts, and over thought death exercises no
solution of continuity. If one dies one's actions cease, one's problem continues. For that reason it is only in so far as I am a man of
action that I shall be dying. You understand what I mean—for I
do not mean that it is my actions that have killed me. It is simply because I have taken refuge from my thoughts in action, and
because after April 5 that refuge will be closed to me, that I take
refuge in a final action which, properly speaking, is neither action
nor refuge.

And perhaps I am no man of action at all, since the action in
which I have taken refuge is properly speaking no action at all,
but merely the expression of a frame of mind. I have gambled,
that is to say I have not speculated. For the speculator acts for
gain: the gambler in order to interest himself. I have gambled—to
escape from you: I have tried to escape from my thoughts of you
into divining the undivinable future. For that is what gambling is.
You try for a rise: you try for a fall—and the rise or the fall may
depend on the momentary madness of a dozen men who declare a
war, or upon the rain from heaven which causes so many more
stalks of wheat to arise upon so many million square inches of
earth. The point is that you make yourself dependent upon
caprice—upon the caprice of the weather or upon the movement
in the minds of men more insane than yourself.

Today I have entered upon what is the biggest gamble of my
whole life. Certain men who believe in me—they are not Edward
Burdens, nevertheless they believe in me—have proposed to me to
form a corner in a certain article which is indispensable to the
daily life of the City. I do not tell you what it is because you will
assuredly witness the effects of this inspiration.

You will say that, when this is accomplished, it will be utterly uninteresting. And that is literally true: when it is done it will be uninteresting. But in the multiplicity of things that will have to be done before the whole thing is done—in the waiting for things to take effect, in the failures perhaps more than in the successes, since the failures will imply new devising—in all the meticulous thought-readings that will be necessary, the interest will lie, and in the men with whom one is brought into contact, the men with whom one struggles, the men whom one must bribe or trick.

And you will say: How can I who am to die in fourteen days embark upon an enterprise that will last many months or many years? That, I think, is very simple.

It is my protest against being called a man of action, the misconception that I have had to resent all my life. And this is a thought: not an action: a thought made up of an almost infinite number of erring calculations. You have probably forgotten that I have founded two towns, upon the south coast: originated four railways in tropical climates and one in the west of England: and opened up heaven knows how many mines of one kind or another —and upon my soul I have forgotten these things too until I began to cast about in my mind. And now I go to my death unmindful of these glories in so far as they are concrete. In that sense my death is utter: it is a solution. But, in so far as they are my refuges from you they remain problems to which, if my ghost is to escape you, I must return again and again.

In dying I surrender to you and thus, for the inner self of myself, death is no ending but the commencement of who knows what tortures. It is only in the latent hope that death is the negation of consciousness that I shall take my life. For death, though it can very certainly end no problem, may at least make us unconscious of how, eventually, the problem solves itself. That, you see, is really the crux of the whole thing—that is why the man of action will take refuge in death: the man of thought, never. But I, I am the man of neither the one nor the other: I am the man of love, which partakes of action and of thought, but which is neither.

The lover, perhaps, the eternal doubter—simply because there is no certain panacea for love. Travel may cure it—but travel may cause to arise homesickness, which of all forms of love is the most terrible. To mix with many other men may cure it—but again, to the man who really loves, it may be a cause for still more terrible unrest, since seeing other men and women may set one always comparing the beloved object with the same thing. And, indeed, the form that it takes with me—for with me love takes the form of a desire to discuss—the form which it takes with me renders each thing that I see, each man with whom I speak, the more torturing, since always I desire to adjust my thoughts of them by your thoughts. I went down the other day—before I had begun to write these letters to you and before I knew death impended so early over me—to the sea at P————. I was trying to get rid of you. I sat in the moonlight and saw the smacks come home, visible for a minute in the track of the moon and then no more than their lights in the darkness. The fishermen talked of death by drowning mostly: the passage of the boats across that trail of light suggested reflections, no doubt trite. But, without you to set my thoughts by, I could get no more forward: I went round and round in a ring from the corpses fished up in the nets to the track of the moon. And since walking up and down on the parade brought me no nearer to you, I did not even care to move: I neither meditated nor walked, neither thought nor acted. And that is real torture.

It was the next morning that I heard that young Burden desired that his fiancée's solicitors should scrutinise the accounts of the Burden Trust—and Death looked up before me.

You will ask: why Death? Why not some alternative? Flight or prison? Well: prison would be an unendurable travelling through Time; flight, an equally unendurable travelling through Time with Space added. Both these things are familiar: Death alone, in spite of all the experience that humanity has had of Death, is the utterly unfamiliar. For a gambler it is a coup alluring beyond belief—as we know neither what we stake nor what we stand to win. I, personally, stand to win a great deal, since Life holds nothing for me and I stake only my life—and what I seek is only forgetfulness of you, or some sort of eventual and incomprehensible union with you. For the union with you that I seek is a queer sort of thing; hardly at all, I think, a union of the body, but a sort of consciousness of our thoughts proceeding onwards together. That we may find in the unending Afterwards. Or we may find the Herb Oblivion.

Either of these things I desire. For, in so far as we can dogmatise about Death we may lay it down that Death is the negation of Action but is powerless against Thought. I do not desire Action: and at the same time I do not fear Thought. For it is not my thoughts of you that I fear: left alone with them I can say: "What is she more than any other material object?" It is my feelings that wear out my brain—my feelings that make me know that you are more than every material object living or still, and more than every faith dead or surviving. For feeling is neither Thought nor Action: it is the very stuff of Life itself. And, if Death be the negation of Life it may well be the end of consciousness.

The worst that Death can do to me is to deliver up for ever to unsatisfied longings for you. Well, that is all that Life has done, that is all that Life can do, for me.

But Life can do so much more that is worse. Believe me when I say that I dread imprisonment—and believe me when I say that I do not dread disgrace. For you know very well that it is true when I say that I positively chuckle at the thought of the shock my fall would give to all these unawakened intelligences of this world. You know how I despise Edward Burden for trusting in me; you know how I have always despised other people who trusted in established reputations. I don't mean to say that I should not have liked to keep the game up, certainly I should, since in gambling it is more desirable to win than to lose. And it is more amusing to fool fools than to give them eye-openers. But I think that, in gambling, it is only a shade less desirable, per se, to lose than to win. The main point is the sensation of either; and the only valid objection to losing is that, if one loses too often, one has at last no longer the wherewithal to gamble. Similarly, to give people eye-openers is, per se, nearly as desirable as to fool them. It is not quite so desirable, since the game itself *is* the fooling. But the great objection in *my* case is that the eye-opener would once and for all put an end to the chance of my ever fooling them again. That, however, is a very small matter and what I dread is not that. If people no longer trusted in me I could no doubt still find an outlet for my energies with those who sought to take advantage of my abilities, trusting to themselves to wrest from me a sufficient share of the plunder that they so ardently desire, that I so really have no use for.

No, I seek in Death a refuge from exposure not because expo-

sure would cripple my energies; it would probably help them: and
not because exposure would mean disgrace; I should probably
find ironical satisfaction in it—but simply because it would mean
imprisonment. That I dread beyond belief: I clench my finger
when, in conversation, I hear the words: "A long sentence." For
that would mean my being delivered up for a long time—for ever
—to you. I write "for ever" advisedly and after reflection, since a
long subjection, without relief, to that strain would leave upon my
brain a wound that must prove ineffaceable. For to be alone and
to think—those are my terrors.

One reads that men who have been condemned for long years
to solitary imprisonment go mad. But I think that even that sad
gift from Omnipotent Fate would not be mine. As I figure the
world to myself, Fate is terrible only to those who surrender to
her. If I surrendered, to the extent of living to go to prison, then
assuredly the future must be uniformly heavy, uniformly doomed,
in my eyes. For I would as soon be mad as anything else I can
think of. But I should not go mad. Men go mad because of the
opportunities they miss; because the world changes outside their
prison walls, or because their children starve. But I have no opportunities to miss or take: the changes of the world to me are
nothing, and there is no soul between whom and starvation I
could stand.

Whilst I am about making this final disposition of my properties
—let me tell you finally what I have done in regard to your husband himself. It is a fact—and this I have been keeping up my
sleeve as a final surprise for you—that he is almost cured. . . .

But I have just received an incomprehensible note from Edward
Burden. He asks me for some particulars as to his confounded estate and whether I can lend him some thousands of pounds at
short notice. Heaven knows what new scrape this is that he's in.
Of course this may precipitate my crash. But whatever happens, I
shall find time to write my final words to you—and nothing else
really matters. . . .

VII

I haven't yet discovered what Edward Burden is doing. I have
found him a good round sum upon mortgage—the irony of the

position being that the money is actually his whilst the mortgage does not actually exist. He says that what he is doing with the money will please me. I suppose that means that he's embarking upon some sort of speculation which he imagines that I would favour. It is odd that he should think that I find gratification in his imitating myself.

But why should I concern myself with this thing at all? Nothing in the world can ever please or displease me any more. For I have taken my resolve: this is my last night upon earth. When I lay down this pen again, I shall never take up any pen more. For I have said all that I can say to you. I am utterly tired out. Tonight I shall make up into a parcel all these letters—I must sit through the night because it is only tomorrow morning that I shall be able to register the parcel to you—and registering it will be my last act upon the habitable globe. For biting through the glass in the ring will be not in action, but the commencement of a new train of thought. Or perhaps only my final action will come to an end when you read these words in Rome. Or will that be only thought—the part of me that lives—pleading to you to give your thoughts for company. I feel too tired to think the matter out!

Let me, then, finish with this earth: I told you, when I finished writing last night, that Robert is almost cured. I would not have told you this for the sake of arrogating to myself the position of a saviour. But I imagine that you would like the cure to go on and, in the case of some accident after my death, it might go all to pieces once more. Quite simply then: I have been doing two things. In the first place I have persuaded your chemists to reduce very gradually the strength of chloral, so that the bottles contain nearly half water. And Robert perceives no difference. Now of course it is very important that he shall not know of the trick that is being so beneficently played on him—so that, in case he should go away or for one reason or another change his chemists, it must be carefully seen to that instead of pure chloral he obtains the exactly diluted mixture. In this way he may be brought gradually to drinking almost pure water.

But that alone would hardly be satisfactory: a comparatively involuntary cure is of little value in comparison with an effort of the will. You may, conceivably, expel nature with a fork, but nothing but a passion will expel a passion. The only point to be proved is whether there exists in your husband any other passion for the sake of which he might abandon his passion for the clearness of vision which he always says his chloral gives him. He has not, of course, the incentives usual to men: you cannot, in fact, "get" him along ordinary lines. . . . But apart from his physical craving for the drug he *has* that passion for clearness of intellect that he says the drug gives him—and it is through that, that at last I have managed to hit his pride.

For I have put it to him very strongly that one view of life is just as good as another—no better, no worse, but just the same. And I have put it to him that his use of chloral simply limits for him the number of views of life that he might conceivably have. And, when you come to think of all the rhapsodies of his that we have listened to, I think that that piece of special pleading is sufficiently justified. I do indeed honestly believe that, for what it is worth, he is on the road to salvation. He means to make a struggle—to attempt the great feat of once more seeing life with the eyes that Fate originally gave to him.

This is my legacy to *you:* if you ask me why I have presented you with this man's new identity—since it *will* mean a new identity—I must answer that I simply don't know. Why have we kept him alive all these years? I have done it no doubt because I had nothing to give you. But you? If you have loved me you must have wished him—I won't say dead—but no more there. Yet you have tried too—and I suppose this answer to the riddle is simply the answer to the whole riddle of our life. We have tried to play a supremely difficult game simply because it sanctified our love. For, after all, sanctification arises from difficulties. Well, we have made our way very strait and we have so narrowed the door of entrance that it has vanished altogether. We have never had *any* hope of a solution that could have satisfied us. If we had cared to break the rules of the game, I suppose we could have done it easily enough —and we could have done it the more easily since neither you nor I ever subscribed to those rules. If we have not it was, I think, simply because we sought the difficulty which sanctifies. . . . Has it been a very imbecile proceeding? I am most uncertain. For it is not a thing to be very proud of—to be able to say that for a whole lifetime one has abstained from that which one most desired. On the other hand, we have won a curious and difficult game. Well—there it is—and there is your legacy. I do not think that there is anything else for me to write about. You will see that, in my will, I have left everything I possess to—Edward Burden. This is not because I wish to make him reparation, and it's not because I wish to avoid scandal: it is simply because it may show him—one very simple thing. It will show him how very nearly I might have made things come right. I have been balancing my accounts very carefully, and I find that, reckoning things reasonably against myself, Edward Burden will have a five-pound note with which to buy himself a mourning-ring.

The being forced to attend to my accounts will make him gasp a good deal. It will certainly shake his belief in all accepted reputations—for he will look on the faces of many men, each "as solid as the Bank of England," and he will think: "I wonder if you are like—?" His whole world will crumble—not because I have been dishonest, since he is coldblooded enough to believe that all men may be dishonest. But he will tremble because I have been able to be so wildly dishonest and yet to be so successfully respectable. He won't even dare to "expose" me, since, if he did that, half of the shares which he will inherit from me would suffer an eclipse of disreputability, would tumble to nothingness in value—and would damage his poor pocket. He will have to have my estate set down at a high figure; he will have to be congratulated on his fortunate inheritance, and he will have, sedulously, to compound my felony.

You will wonder how I can be capable of this final cruelty—the most cruel thing that, perhaps, ever one man did to another. I will tell you why it is: it is because I hate all the Edward Burdens of the world—because, being the eternal Haves of the world, they have made their idiotic rules of the game. And you and I suffer: you and I, the eternal Have Nots. And we suffer, not because their rules bind us, but because, being the finer spirits, we are forced to set ourselves rules that are still more strict in order that, in all things, we may be the truly gallant.

But why do I write: "You will wonder how I can be capable of this." You will have understood—you who understand everything.

Eight in the morning. Well: now we part. I am going to register the parcel containing all these letters to you. We part: and it is as if you were dropping back—the lost Eurydice of the world—into an utter blackness. For, in a minute, you will be no more than part of my past. Well then: goodnight.

VIII

You will have got the telegram I sent you long before you got the parcel of letters: you will have got the note I wrote you by the same post as the letters themselves. If I have taken these three days to myself before again writing to you it has been because I have needed to recover my power of thinking. Now, in a way, I have recovered it—and it is only fair to say that I have devoted all my thoughts to how the new situation affects you—and you in your relations to me.

It places me in your hands—let that be written first and foremost. You have to decree my life or my death. For I take it that now we can never get back again into our old position: I have spoken, you have heard me speak. The singular unity, the silence of our old life is done with for good. There is perhaps no reason why this should not be so: silence is no necessary part of our relationship. But it has seemed to make a rather exquisite bond between us.

It must, if I am to continue to live—it must be replaced by some other bond. In our silence we have seemed to speak in all sorts of strange ways: we have perhaps read each other's thoughts. I have seen words form themselves upon your lips. But now you must—there is no way out of it—you *must* write to me. You must write to me fully: all your thoughts. You must, as I have done, find the means of speech—or I can no longer live. . . .

I am reprieved!

I don't know if, in my note to you, I explained exactly what had happened. It was in this way. I was anxious to be done with my world very early and, as soon as eight o'clock struck, I set out for the post office at the corner to register that parcel of letters for you. Till the task was accomplished—the last I was to perform on earth—I noticed nothing: I was simply in a hurry. But, having given the little fagot into the hands of a sleepy girl, I said to myself suddenly: "Now I *am* dead!" I began suddenly, as they say of young children, to "notice." A weight that I had never felt before seemed to fall away from me. I noticed, precisely, that the girl clerk was sleepy, that, as she reached up one hand to take the parcel over the brass caging, she placed the other over her mouth to hide a yawn.

And out on the pavement it was most curious what had befallen the world. It had lost all interest: but it had become fascinating, vivid. I had not, you see, any senses left, but my eyesight and hearing. Vivid: that is the word. I watched a newsboy throw his papers down an area, and it appeared wonderfully interesting to discover that *that* was how one's papers got into the house. I watched a milkman go up some doorsteps to put a can of milk beside a boot-scraper and I was wonderfully interested to see a black cat follow him. They were the clearest moments I have ever spent upon the earth—those when I was dead. They were so clear because nothing else weighed on my attention but just those little things. It was an extraordinary, a luxuriant feeling. That, I imagine, must have been how Adam and Eve felt before they had eaten of the fruit of knowledge.

Supposing I had tacitly arranged with myself that I would die in the street, I think I should still have walked home simply to dally longer with that delightful feeling of sheer curiosity. For it was sheer curiosity to see how this world, which I had never looked at, really performed before utterly unbiassed eyes.

That was why, when I got home, I sent away the messenger that brought to me Edward Burden's letter; there was to be no answer. Whatever Burden's query might be I was not going to commit myself to any other act. My last was that of sending off the parcel to you.

My opening Burden's letter when the messenger had gone was simply a part of my general curiosity. I wanted to see how a Burden letter would look when it no longer had any bearings at all for me. It was as if I were going to read a letter from that dear Edward to a man I did not know upon a subject of which I had never heard.

And then I was reprieved!

The good Edward, imagining that I was seriously hurt at his having proposed to allow his wife's solicitors to superintend my stewardship—the good Edward in his concern had positively insisted that all the deeds should be returned to me absolutely unchecked. He said that he had had a hard fight for it and that the few thousands he had borrowed from me had represented his settlement, which he had thus paid in specie. . . .

It chimed in wonderfully with his character, when I come to think of it. Of course he was disciplining Miss Averies' representatives just as he had disciplined herself in the matter of China tea of which I have written to you. And he had imagined that I was seriously hurt! Can you figure to yourself such an imbecile?

But, if you permit me to continue to live, you will be saving the poor fool from the great shock I had prepared for him—the avalanche of discovery, the earthquake of uncertainty. For he says in that so kind way of his that, having thus shown his entire confidence in me—in the fact that Providence is on the side of all Burdens—he will choose a time in the future, convenient for me, when he will go thoroughly with me into his accounts. And inasmuch as his wedding tour will take him all around the world, I have at least a year in which to set things straight. And of course I can put off his scrutiny indefinitely or deceive him for ever.

I did not think all these things at once. In fact, when I had read his letter, so strong within me was the feeling that it was only a mental phenomenon, a thing that had no relation with me—the feeling of finality was so strong upon me that I actually found myself sitting in that chair before I realized what had occurred.

What had occurred was that I had become utterly and for good your property.

In that sense only am I reprieved. As far as Edward Burden is concerned I am entirely saved. I stand before you and ask you to turn your thumb up or down. For, having spoken as I have to you, I have given you a right over me. Now that the pressing necessity for my death is over I have to ask you whether I shall plunge into new adventures that will lead me to death or whether I am to find some medium in which we may lead a life of our own, in some way together. I was about to take my life to avoid prison: now prison is no more a part of my scheme of existence. But I must now have some means of working towards you or I must run some new and wild risk to push you out of my thoughts. I don't, as you know, ask you to be my secret mistress, I don't ask you to elope with me. But I say that you *must* belong to me as

much in thought as I have, in this parcel of letters, been revealed
and given over to you. Otherwise, I must once more gamble—and
having tasted of gambling in the shadow of death, I must gamble
for ever in that way. I must, I mean, feel that I am coming towards you or committing crimes that I may forget you.

My dear, I am a very tired man. If you know what it was to
long for you as I have longed for you all these years, you would
wonder that I did not, sitting in that chair, put the ring up to my
teeth, in spite of Burden's letter, and end it. I have an irresistible
longing for rest—or perhaps it is only your support. To think that
I must face for ever—or for as long as it lasts—this troublesome
excitement of avoiding thoughts of you—that was almost unbear-
able. I resisted because I had written these letters to you. I love
you and I know you love me—yet without them I would have in-
flicted upon you the wound of my death. Having written them I
cannot face the cruelty to you. I mean that, if I had died without
your knowing why, it would have been only a death grievous to
you—still it is the duty of humanity and of you with humanity to
bear and to forget deaths. But now that you must know, I could not
face the cruelty of filling you with the pain of unmerited remorse.
For I know you would have felt remorse, and it would have been
unmerited since I gave you no chance or any time to stretch out
your hands to me. Now I give it you and wait for your verdict.

For the definite alternatives are these: I will put Burden's estate
absolutely clear within the year and work out, in order to make
safe money, the new and comparatively sober scheme of which I
have written to you: that I will do if you will consent to be mine
to the extent of sharing our thoughts alone. Or, if you will not, I
will continue to gamble more widely than ever with the Burden
money. And that in the end means death and a refuge from you.

So then, I stand reprieved—and the final verdict is in your
hands.

Biographical Bibliography

The following biographical bibliography consists, apart from a few most important dates in Joseph Conrad's life, of a list of all his novels, short stories, and longer essays, arranged in the order of their composition. The dates given are based exclusively on available documents. Thus, although Conrad maintains in a letter to Pinker, dated 19 January 1922, that he wrote "The Black Mate" as early as in 1886, I discount this statement, as there is no evidence to support his claim. Basically, two kinds of documents are taken into consideration: references in letters (Conrad's letters to J. B. Pinker, his literary agent, written after 1900, are particularly valuable) and earliest publications. The only exception is made with respect to the date when Conrad began *Almayer's Folly:* here I follow Conrad's own report in *A Personal Record*. Whenever the exact date is doubtful, I add a question mark. Of course, there frequently remains the possibility that a particular piece had been begun earlier than it was ever mentioned; this seems to be the case with *Lord Jim*. Full documentation for all entries is given in my forthcoming biography of Conrad, to be published by Rutgers University Press in 1979.

1857

3 December Jósef Teodor Konrad Korzeniowski born in Berdyczów (today Berdichiv) in the Ukraine, son of Apollo Nałęcz Korzeniowski, Polish writer and estate manager, and of Ewa née Bobrowska

1861

21 October	Apollo Korzeniowski arrested in Warsaw by Russian police for underground patriotic activities.

1862

9 May	The Korzeniowskis are both sentenced to exile and sent under escort to Vologda in Russia. Their son accompanies them.

1865

18 April	Ewa Korzeniowska dies of tuberculosis.

1868

January	Apollo Korzeniowski, seriously ill, is reprieved and leaves Russia with his son.

1869

23 May	Apollo Korzeniowski dies in Cracow.

1874

26 September	Konrad Korzeniowski (he always used his third given name as the first and never legally changed his names) leaves Poland for Marseilles.

1878

11 July	joins his first English ship the *Skimmer of the Sea*

1886

19 August	becomes a British subject
11 November	passes his examination for Ordinary Master of the British merchant marine

1889

2 July	released from Russian citizenship
autumn	according to his own reminiscences begins *Almayer's Folly*

1890

March	the earliest evidence of the existence of the first chapters of *Almayer's Folly*
12 June–4 December	works in the Belgian Congo for the Société Anonyme pour le Commerce du Haut-Congo

1894

17 January	leaves his last position as a seaman
24 April	finishes the draft of *Almayer's Folly*
August	begins *Two Vagabonds* (later renamed *An Outcast of the Islands*)
3 September	the manuscript of *Almayer's Folly* accepted by T. Fisher Unwin in London

1895

29 April	*Almayer's Folly—A Story of an Eastern River* pub-

lished. Korzeniowski adopts "Joseph Conrad" as his pen name.

16 September	finishes *An Outcast of the Islands*
late autumn(?)	begins *The Sisters*

1896

4 March	*An Outcast of the Islands* published
March	*The Sisters* laid aside never to be completed
24 March	marries Miss Jessie George born 22 February 1873
end of March	begins *The Rescuer* (later renamed *The Rescue*)
May	writes "The Idiots"
June(?)	begins *The Nigger of the "Narcissus"*
21 July	finishes "An Outpost of Progress" (originally "A Victim of Progress")
August	*The Rescue* put aside; writes "The Lagoon"
October	writing *The Nigger of the "Narcissus"*

1897

17(?) January	finishes *The Nigger of the "Narcissus"*
February	begins "Karain, a Memory"
14 April	finishes "Karain"
May(?)	begins "The Return"
24 August	finishes the Preface to *The Nigger of the "Narcissus"*
August	takes up *The Rescue*
24 September	finishes "The Return"
2 December	*The Nigger of the "Narcissus"—A Tale of the Sea* published

1898

26 March	*Tales of Unrest* ("Karain," "The Idiots," "An Outpost of Progress," "The Return," "The Lagoon") published
May(?)	begins *Lord Jim* (the earliest draft bears the title *Tuan Jim—A Sketch*)
3 June	finishes "Youth"
November	beginning of collaboration with Ford Madox Hueffer (later F. M. Ford) on *Romance* (initially *Seraphina*)
December	again puts *The Rescue* aside
December	begins "Heart of Darkness"

1899

6 February	finishes "Heart of Darkness"
November	collaborates with Ford Madox Hueffer on *The Inheritors*

1900

16 March	Conrad and Hueffer finish *The Inheritors*

14 July	completes *Lord Jim*
July	again collaborates with Ford on *Romance*
September	begins "Typhoon"
15 October	*Lord Jim—A Tale* published

1901

11 January	finishes "Typhoon"
January(?)	begins "Falk"
May	finishes "Falk," begins "Amy Foster" (earlier titles: "A Husband," "A Castaway")
May–June	Conrad works on *Romance*
18 June	finishes "Amy Foster"
26 June	*The Inheritors—An Extravagant Story* published
December	the final stage of the work on *Romance* begins

1902

16 February	finishes "Tomorrow"
March	begins *Nostromo* and "The End of the Tether"
March	Conrad and Hueffer finish *Romance*
May	first projects of *The Mirror of the Sea*
15 October	finishes "The End of the Tether" (initially "The End of the Song")
13 November	*Youth and Two Other Stories* ("Youth," "Heart of Darkness," "The End of the Tether") published

1903

22 April	*Typhoon and Other Stories* ("Typhoon," "Amy Foster," "Falk," "Tomorrow") published
16 October	*Romance—A Novel* published
November	another brief attempt at continuing *The Rescue*

1904

January	begins *The Mirror of the Sea*
30 August	completes *Nostromo*
October	begins "Benavides" (later renamed "Strong Man," finally called "Gaspar Ruiz")
14 October	*Nostromo—A Tale of the Seaboard* published

1905

14 January–23 April	writes "Autocracy and War" (initially entitled "The Council of Europe")
April	begins *Dynamite* (or *Dynamite Ship,* finally called *Chance*)
6 October	completes *The Mirror of the Sea*
October(?)	finishes "Gaspar Ruiz"
December	finishes "An Anarchist"
27 December	begins "The Informer"

1906

1 January	finishes "The Informer"

January(?)	writes "The Brute"
21 February	begins *The Secret Agent* (originally *Verloc*)
May–October	with Conrad's help, Ford writes *The Nature of a Crime*
4 October	*The Mirror of the Sea—Memories and Impressions* published
November	finishes *The Secret Agent*
4 December	finishes "Il Conde"

1907

January	for a short time resumes work on *Chance*
January	begins "The Duel"
11 April	finishes "The Duel"
12 September	*The Secret Agent—A Simple Tale* published
December	begins *Razumov* (later renamed *Under Western Eyes*)

1908

January–February	writes "The Black Mate"
6 August	*A Set of Six* ("Gaspar Ruiz," "The Informer," "The Brute," "An Anarchist," "The Duel," "Il Conde") published
September	begins *A Personal Record* (originally *Some Reminiscences*)
December	interrupts writing *A Personal Record*

1909

| *end November–* *beginning December* | writes "The Secret Sharer" (initially called "The Secret Self" or "The Other Self") |

1910

22 January	completes *Under Western Eyes*
18 May	begins "A Smile of Fortune"
1 September	finishes "A Smile of Fortune"
24 September	finishes "Prince Roman"
October	begins "The Partner"
December	finishes "The Partner"
26 December	begins "Freya of the Seven Isles"

1911

28 February	finishes "Freya of the Seven Isles"
May	resumes work on *Chance*
5 October	*Under Western Eyes* published

1912

| *19 January* | *Some Reminiscences* (later renamed *A Personal Record*) published |
| *25 March* | completes *Chance* |

early May	begins *The Dollars* (later renamed *An Island Story,* finally *Victory*)
14 October	*"Twixt Land and Sea—Tales* ("A Smile of Fortune," "The Secret Sharer," "Freya of the Seven Islands") published
December	begins "The Inn of the Two Witches"

1913

February(?)	finishes "The Inn of the Two Witches"
18 September	*Chance—A Tale in Two Parts* published in a limited edition
November	begins "The Planter of Malata" (initially entitled "The Assistant")
14 December	"The Planter of Malata" completed
December	"Because of the Dollars" (earlier titles: "The Dollars," "The Spoiled Smile") begun

1914

early January	"Because of the Dollars" finished
15 January	regular edition of *Chance*
28 June	completes *Victory*
25 July	leaves with his family for holiday in Poland; stranded there by the outbreak of war, returns to England 3 November

1915

24 February	*Within the Tides—Tales* ("The Planter of Malata," "The Inn of Two Witches," "Because of the Dollars") published
February	begins *The First Command* (later renamed *The Shadow Line*)
27 March	*Victory—An Island Tale* published
17 December	completes *The Shadow Line*

1916

February–March	writes "The Warrior's Soul" (initially entitled "The Humane Tomassov")
30 October	finishes "The Tale"

1917

19 March	*The Shadow Line—A Confession* published
late July	begins *The Arrow of Gold* (early titles: *R.T.— Selected Passages from Letters; R.T.—Fragments; Lost Arrow*)

1918

14 June	completes *The Arrow of Gold*
early July	resumes his work on *The Rescue*

12 December	finishes "The Crime of Partition"
	1919
25 May	completes *The Rescue*
6 August	*The Arrow of Gold—A Story Between Two Notes* published
	1920
15 March	finishes a dramatic adaptation of *The Secret Agent,* begun in October 1919
May	begins *Suspense* (initially *The Isle of Rest*)
21 May	*The Rescue—A Romance of the Shallows* published
14 September–late October	works on *Gaspar the Strong Man,* film script based on "Gaspar Ruiz"
9 October	ends preparing the volume *Notes on Life and Letters*
	1921
25 March	*Notes on Life and Letters* published
June	translates Bruno Winawer's *Księga Hioba* from Polish: *The Book of Job*
9 October	begins *The Rover*
	1922
27 June	finishes *The Rover,* then expanded to sixteen chapters by 16 July
	1923
12–23 March	writes "Stephen Crane"
1 May–2 June	on the invitation of Frank Nelson Doubleday, visits the United States (New York and Boston)
1–12 November	writes "Geography and Some Explorers"
1 December	*The Rover* published
	1924
26 May	declines a knighthood offered him by H. M. Government
3 August	dies of heart attack at his home, Oswalds, in Bishopsbourne, near Canterbury
26 September	*The Nature of a Crime* published
	1925
23 January	*Tales of Hearsay* ("The Warrior's Soul," "Prince Roman," "The Tale," "The Black Mate") published
15 September	*Suspense* published
	1926
3 March	*Last Essays* published
	1928
January	*The Sisters* published